Mindfulness
IN THE
Classroom

33 - mindful breathing
34 - Anger · thoughts are not facts
37-40 - other formal (M) activities
41 - (M) helps with transitioning in ES
45 - (M) takeaways

Other ASCD Books by
Thomas Armstrong

ADD/ADHD Alternatives in the Classroom

Awakening Genius in the Classroom

*The Best Schools: How Human Development Research
Should Inform Educational Practice*

Multiple Intelligences in the Classroom, 4th ed.

*The Multiple Intelligences of Reading and Writing:
Making the Words Come Alive*

*Neurodiversity in the Classroom: Strength-Based Strategies to
Help Students with Special Needs Succeed in School and Life*

*The Power of the Adolescent Brain: Strategies for
Teaching Middle and High School Students*

ASCD MEMBER BOOK

Many ASCD members received this book as a
member benefit upon its initial release.

Learn more at: **www.ascd.org/memberbooks**

Mindfulness

IN THE

Classroom

Strategies for Promoting Concentration, Compassion, and Calm

THOMAS ARMSTRONG

Alexandria, Virginia USA

1703 N. Beauregard St. • Alexandria, VA 22311-1714 USA
Phone: 800-933-2723 or 703-578-9600 • Fax: 703-575-5400
Website: www.ascd.org • E-mail: member@ascd.org
Author guidelines: www.ascd.org/write

Ronn Nozoe, *Interim CEO and Executive Director;* Stefani Roth, *Publisher;* Genny Ostertag, *Director, Content Acquisitions;* Julie Houtz, *Director, Book Editing & Production;* Darcie Russell, *Editor;* Judi Connelly, *Senior Art Director;* Melissa Johnston, *Graphic Designer;* Keith Demmons, *Senior Production Designer;* Mike Kalyan, *Director, Production Services;* Trinay Blake, *E-Publishing Specialist*

All web links in this book are correct as of the publication date below but may have become inactive or otherwise modified since that time. If you notice a deactivated or changed link, please e-mail books@ascd.org with the words "Link Update" in the subject line. In your message, please specify the web link, the book title, and the page number on which the link appears.

PAPERBACK ISBN: 978-1-4166-2794-4   ASCD product #120018
PDF E-BOOK ISBN: 978-1-4166-2796-8; see Books in Print for other formats.
Quantity discounts are available: e-mail programteam@ascd.org or call 800-933-2723, ext. 5773, or 703-575-5773. For desk copies, go to www.ascd.org/deskcopy.

ASCD Member Book No. FY19-8A (Jul 2019 PSI+). ASCD Member Books mail to Premium (P), Select (S), and Institutional Plus (I+) members on this schedule: Jan, PSI+; Feb, P; Apr, PSI+; May, P; Jul, PSI+; Aug, P; Sep, PSI+; Nov, PSI+; Dec, P. For current details on membership, see www.ascd.org/membership.

Library of Congress Cataloging-in-Publication Data

Names: Armstrong, Thomas, author.
Title: Mindfulness in the classroom : strategies for promoting concentration, compassion, and calm / Thomas Armstrong.
Description: Alexandria, Virginia, USA : ASCD, [2019] | Includes bibliographical references and index.
Identifiers: LCCN 2019014631 (print) | LCCN 2019020080 (ebook) | ISBN 9781416627968 (Pdf) | ISBN 9781416627944 (pbk. : alk. paper)
Subjects: LCSH: Affective education. | Reflective teaching. | Mindfulness (Psychology)
Classification: LCC LB1072 (ebook) | LCC LB1072 .A75 2019 (print) | DDC 370.15/34--dc23
LC record available at https://lccn.loc.gov/2019014631

29 28 27 26 25 24 23 22 21 20 19   1 2 3 4 5 6 7 8 9 10 11 12

Mindfulness

IN THE

Classroom

Preface

Thirty years ago I took an eight-week class in mindfulness meditation from clinical psychologist Jack Kornfield, author of several best-selling books on mindfulness. At the time, I was in the midst of a major depressive episode and sought assistance from this practice in combatting my mood disorder. After a few weeks of meditating, my depression gradually began to lift (research 15 years later would support the use of mindfulness meditation in effectively treating depressive illnesses like mine). Years later, as my practice became more sporadic, I had a relapse of my depression, and this time I was more careful and made sure to do at least 30 minutes of mindfulness practice each day. That was almost 10 years ago, and since then I've been depression free. I plan to practice mindfulness every day for the rest of my life.

Since that time, mindfulness has taken off as a popular method of personal and professional transformation. Thousands of studies conducted throughout the past 20 years have demonstrated the effectiveness of mindfulness in treating a wide range of disorders, including depression, anxiety, post-traumatic stress disorder, eating disorders, chronic pain, and even psychosis.

More recently the focus has turned to schools and well-designed randomized controlled studies are highlighting the value of mindfulness practices in improving students' executive functioning, bolstering working memory, supporting social and emotional development, and reducing stress levels. Although the scientific study of mindfulness in the schools is still in its infancy, with several long-term studies in progress, there now is growing evidence supporting the use of mindfulness to enhance concentration, compassion, and calm in the classroom. See Appendix A for a useful glossary of neuroscience terms.

As I did the research for this book, I encountered the word *mindfulness* used in reference to a wide collection of interventions including mood lighting, relaxation strategies, jumping on a trampoline, stress-reducing coloring books, guided visualizations, chanting, and other body-mind activities. None of these are true examples of mindfulness—at least in the way that I'll be using the term in this book. I also encountered confusion of the word *mindfulness* with the ideas of Harvard professor Ellen Langer (2014), who uses it in reference to thinking "outside of the box."

In this book, I'll be using the word *mindfulness* in a very precise way. Mindfulness, simply put, is *the intentional focus of one's attention on the present moment in a nonjudgmental way*. The concept of mindfulness has roots in Buddhism, especially Theravada Buddhism, which is predominant in Southeast Asia. However, my own reference point for the *secular* foundation of mindfulness comes from the work of biologist Jon Kabat-Zinn (2013). In the 1970s at the University of Massachusetts Medical School, Kabat-Zinn developed a method for treating chronic pain and stress through an eight-week course that he referred to as Mindfulness-Based Stress Reduction (MBSR). The vast majority of scientific studies on mindfulness over the past two decades have been based on this program and a related one called Mindfulness-Based Cognitive Therapy (MBCT), which combines mindfulness experiences with standard cognitive-behavioral therapy. Although the application of mindfulness to the schools, and to students at different ages, requires many significant changes, adaptations, and modifications (these will be discussed in Chapter 6), many of the activities that I write about (especially those described in Chapter 3) owe their origins to Kabat-Zinn's MBSR program and to my own experiences practicing mindfulness over the past 30 years.

It's important for me to state from the outset that this book is not a formal program for implementing mindfulness in the schools or for formally training teachers to use mindfulness in their classrooms. There already are perhaps 30 to 40 programs that do this around the United States and in the United Kingdom and Australia (I list several of these in Appendix B). Such programs vary in the methods they use, the services they provide, and the philosophies they espouse, although most of them adhere to some version of Kabat-Zinn's formulation of mindfulness. This book, on the other hand,

- Provides an overview of mindfulness both as personal practice and as a method to be used in the classroom.
- Details how mindfulness positively affects the brain's structure and function, particularly in regard to its ability to deal with stress.
- Shows how mindfulness fits within existing education models such as Social and Emotional Learning (SEL), Positive Behavioral Interventions and Supports (PBIS), and Universal Design for Learning (UDL).
- Reviews current evidence-based research on the effectiveness of mindfulness for use in the classroom.
- Communicates many of the essential features of mindfulness programs and practices.
- Offers suggestions for how mindfulness can be adapted at different grade levels.
- Provides ways of integrating mindfulness into the regular school curriculum (e.g., in language arts, math, science, social studies).
- Suggests several ways in which mindfulness can be implemented on a schoolwide basis.
- Enumerates guidelines to ensure that mindfulness is taught in the schools in a responsible way (e.g., so that it doesn't violate the separation of church and state in the U.S. Constitution).

The book is designed to meet a wide range of needs for educators with varying backgrounds and levels of experience. *Mindfulness in the Classroom* will appeal to several audiences, including

• Educators who are totally new to the subject of mindfulness, providing them with an overview and tools they need to start their own practice and immediately begin using mindfulness in their classrooms.

• Teachers who have begun using a few mindfulness practices in their classroom and want additional strategies and information for extending the practice.

• Teachers and administrators who have been using mindfulness in their classrooms for some time as part of a formal mindfulness program and are seeking ways to integrate mindfulness further on a schoolwide basis.

• Specialists who are working with at-risk kids or students in special education and want to offer emotional self-regulation strategies and provide activities that will improve executive functioning and reduce stress.

• School counselors and other support personnel who wish to add mindfulness to their tool kit in helping students with emotional and behavioral difficulties.

I want to reiterate that mindfulness is a completely *secular* practice if practiced in accordance with the guidelines discussed in this book (this issue will be explored in depth in Chapter 9). In researching this book, I was a bit alarmed to see the trappings of spirituality penetrating mindfulness practices in some public school classrooms, with kids sitting in the lotus position, using *mudras* (specific placement of the hands while practicing), listening to Tibetan singing bells, and even chanting and receiving "spiritual" instruction (e.g., "the God in me sees the God in you!"). Because the primary readers of this book will be public school educators, I cannot overemphasize the need to err on the side of secularity and make sure that religious or spiritual principles don't seep into the practices. Although the courts thus far have ruled in favor of yoga and mindfulness in the schools (see, for example, Perry, 2015), careless practice will only sow confusion and controversy that could ultimately undermine the entire use of mindfulness in the schools.

My hope is that readers will develop a strong level of confidence in the power of mindfulness practices to open up new potential in their students, leading to greater levels of social, emotional, and cognitive competence. As I point out in the first chapter, we've never experienced times as stressful as they are now, and mindfulness has emerged just in the nick of time to offer students relief and greater levels of resilience in dealing with the pressures associated with this fast-paced, technology-ridden culture of ours. Happy reading, and may all of your moments be mindful ones!

1

Joining the Quiet Revolution

An epidemic is sweeping through our classrooms today. Not connected to a virus, bacteria, or any other pathogen, the malady is stress. Our students are experiencing stress at levels never before seen in the history of U.S. education. The statistics are alarming. Here are a few of them:

• One in 10 preschoolers has had suicidal thoughts (Whalen, Dixon-Gordon, Belden, Barch, & Luby, 2015).

• Doctors are increasingly reporting children in early elementary school suffering from migraine headaches and ulcers, and many physicians see a clear connection to pressure related to school performance (Abeles, 2016).

• A third of our adolescents report feeling depressed or overwhelmed because of stress, and their single biggest source of stress is school (American Psychological Association, 2014).

• Roughly 1 in 4 girls and 1 in 10 boys in U.S. high schools try to harm themselves even when they are not attempting suicide (Monto, McRee, & Deryck, 2018).

• In a Yale University survey of more than 22,000 high school students, teens reported feeling stressed 80 percent of the time in school (Brackett, 2016).

• By age 21, according to one longitudinal study, 82.5 percent of our students will have met the criteria for at least one psychiatric disorder (Copeland, Shanahan, Costello, & Angold, 2011). (No, this is not a misprint.)

Student stress occurs at all levels of the socioeconomic pyramid. Dale Caldwell, former head of school at the Village Charter School in Trenton, New Jersey, uses the phrase "urban traumatic stress disorder" to describe the problem among those living in poverty. A consultant at the school, Trish Miele, talks about the anxiety that plagues these inner-city students: "So much of their life is living on the edge of stress. . . . It could be food insufficiency, it could be general safety, not having a home, it could be abusive. . . . So many things are coming at them in the urban environment" (Buffum, 2017). On the other end of the economic spectrum, students are under tremendous pressure to perform academically. Reflecting on her experience teaching 3rd grade in the wealthy West Windsor–Plainsboro public school district for 10 years, Miele comments, "The district is very high-achieving. . . . I would have kids coming to me when we started doing testing, [saying], 'If I don't do well, I won't get into Princeton!' And I'm like, 'You're eight. What are you worrying about?'" (Buffum, 2017).

The Mindful Solution to Stress

Fortunately, schools are beginning to respond to this epidemic of stress. One intervention that has received a great deal of attention over the past few years is mindfulness: the nonjudgmental awareness of each present moment in time. Although rooted in a thousand-year-old Buddhist tradition, mindfulness was given a solid secular foundation in science through the efforts of biologist Jon Kabat-Zinn, founder of the Stress Reduction Clinic at the University of Massachusetts Medical Center. He created a stress-reduction and chronic pain management program in the early 1970s based upon mindfulness (Kabat-Zinn, 2013). Since that time, more than 3,000 scientific studies have addressed the topic of mindfulness (Regents of the University of California, 2014). These studies have demonstrated the effectiveness of mindfulness practice in treating chronic pain (Garland et al., 2017); high blood pressure (Palta et al., 2012); immune function (Davidson et al., 2003); anxiety (Vøllestad, Sivertsen, & Nielsen, 2011); depression (Kuyken et al., 2008); post-traumatic stress disorder (Possemato et al., 2016); eating disorders (Katterman, Kleinman, Hood, Nackers, & Corsica, 2014); psychosis (Aust & Bradshaw, 2017); substance abuse (Bowen et al., 2014); and a host of other mental and physical ills.

Mindfulness in Popular Culture

As a result of such a strong evidence base, mindfulness has entered popular culture in the United States (as well as in the United Kingdom and Australia). The mindfulness and meditation industry has become a one-billion-dollar-a-year business (Wieczner, 2016). Close to 80 percent of all medical schools in the United States offer some aspect of mindfulness training in their programs (Barnes, Hattan, Black, & Schuman-Olivier, 2017). The National Health Service in the U.K. lists mindfulness as one of its five steps to mental well-being (National Health Service, 2016). Chris Ruane, a member of the British Parliament, has set up a mindfulness training group for its MPs (Booth, 2017), and U.S. Representative Tim Ryan of Ohio has authored a book on mindfulness (Ryan, 2012) and promoted its widespread use among the American electorate.

These examples are just part of the mindfulness revolution. In addition, the U.S. Army has instituted a mindfulness program—Mindfulness-Based Mind Fitness Training (MMFT, pronounced "M-fit")—to improve mental performance and bolster the emotional health of soldiers under the stress and strain of war (Myers, 2015). The National Basketball Association (NBA) has teamed up with Headspace, a leading mindfulness app, to provide mindfulness training to all league and team staff and family members (NBA Communications, 2018). Mindfulness training is used in several Fortune 500 companies, such as Nike, General Mills, Goldman Sachs, Google, and Apple (Levin, 2017). Even *Sesame Street* is using mindfulness principles. In one video created by the Children's Television Workshop, the Count teaches Cookie Monster how to concentrate on his breathing to reduce stress (to watch it, go to https://sesamestreetincommunities.org/activities /count-breathe-relax/).

The Growth of School-Based Mindfulness Programs

The first major effort to use mindfulness in the schools began in the United Kingdom in 2007 with a series of uniform lesson plans delivered in classrooms across the country (Davis, 2015). Over the past decade, several other programs have emerged to deliver mindfulness training in classrooms around the world. They include Mindful Schools, MindUP, Calm Classroom, Inner Explorer, Master Mind, Moment, A Still Quiet Place, Mindful Schools, the Attention Academy, Inward Bound Mindfulness Education, and Learning to Breathe (see Appendix B for contact information on these and other mindfulness programs). MindUP reports reaching over 500,000 students around the world in the past decade, and Mindful Schools says it has reached over 300,000 students in the United States in the past five years (Strauss, 2016).

Although alike in embracing mindfulness, these programs vary considerably. Some offer discrete training classes, whereas others use whole-school or even districtwide immersion models. Program duration runs from four weeks to several years. Some use external facilitators to teach mindfulness, others train a school's teachers to provide these lessons, and still others use no facilitators at all, relying upon audio and video recordings to guide mindfulness sessions. Evaluations of these programs reveal successful implementation, high recruitment and retention rates, positive qualitative feedback from teachers and students, broad program dissemination, and long-term sustainability (Semple, Droutman, & Reid, 2017).

What the Research Says About Mindfulness

A number of school-related research projects are currently underway to gauge the long-term effectiveness of mindfulness training in students. The Jefferson County Public Schools in Louisville, Kentucky, has partnered with the University of Virginia to implement the Compassionate Schools Project, a seven-year, $12 million research project based on mindfulness principles (Marshall, 2017). In the United Kingdom, the University of Oxford has teamed up with University College London and the Medical Research Council in another seven-year project to study the application of mindfulness practice with adolescents in the schools, at a cost of $7.5 million (Mundasad, 2015). In Chicago, the Erikson Institute, a developmentally based graduate school, has been given $3 million by the U.S. Department of Education to study the effectiveness of mindfulness at 30 high-poverty schools encompassing more than 2,000 students in kindergarten through 2nd grade (DeRuy, 2016).

Along with these longitudinal programs, there's been a tsunami of short-term studies on using mindfulness in the schools. These have offered preliminary evidence of the effectiveness of mindfulness with respect to a wide range of important skills necessary for school success, including

- Executive functioning (Flook et al., 2010).
- Sustained attention (Gu, Xu, & Zhu, 2018).
- Working memory (Quach, Jastrowski Mano, & Alexander, 2016).
- Social and emotional development (Schonert-Reichl & Lawlor, 2010).
- Improved math performance (Schonert-Reichl et al., 2015).
- Self-regulation (Viglas & Perlman, 2018).

Interestingly, two of these studies (Flook et al., 2010; Viglas & Perlman, 2018) indicated that mindfulness practices were especially effective with students who had difficulties with executive functioning or self-regulation. Similarly, mindfulness appears to be very effective on a number of levels for low-income minority students in urban settings. One randomized controlled study, for example, published in the prestigious journal *Pediatrics*, showed improvements in urban, at-risk middle school students with respect to somatization (having medical symptoms without any known cause), depression, negative affect, negative coping, rumination, self-hostility, and post-traumatic symptom severity (Sibinga, Webb, Ghazarian, & Ellen, 2016).

There is also emerging research suggesting that mindfulness practices benefit students with special needs. One study of adolescents with autism who went through nine weeks of mindfulness training saw decreases in rumination, as well as improved social responsiveness, social communication, social cognition, and social motivation (de Bruin, Blom, Smit, van Steensel, & Bögels, 2015). A review of several recent studies concluded that mindfulness may prove to be a novel psychosocial intervention for students with ADHD (Cassone, 2015). Mindfulness has shown effectiveness with a group of adolescent psychiatric outpatients displaying a heterogeneous mix of emotional and behavioral disorders. Those students engaged with Mindfulness-Based Stress Reduction (MBSR) self-reported reduced symptoms of anxiety, depression, and somatic distress, and increased self-esteem and sleep quality. Of clinical significance, the MBSR group showed a higher percentage of diagnostic improvement over the course of the five-month program (Biegel, Brown, Shapiro, & Schubert, 2009). A study of students with intellectual disabilities showed that mindfulness practice led to improved task performance and reduced task avoidance (Kim & Kwon, 2018).

As of 2019, there have been three separate meta-analyses of the existing literature on mindfulness in the schools. Although meta-analyses can produce watered-down data due to differences among the studies analyzed, they can also be useful in determining the overall effectiveness of an intervention across a wide range of studies (see Ahn, Ames, & Myers, 2012, for a discussion of strengths and weaknesses of meta-analyses in educational research). In the first meta-analysis, which included 19 studies using control groups (Zenner, Herrnleben-Kurz, & Walach, 2014), overall effect sizes within and between groups was .40 and .41 respectively (using Hedges' g, a measure of effect size). An effect size of .40 is considered to be within the range of desired intervention effects, according to Hattie (2008). The meta-analysis also looked at specific components of desired effects and found a large effect size (.80) in cognitive performance among students in mindfulness studies.

A second meta-analysis (Maynard, Solis, Miller, & Brendel, 2017) demonstrated a small, statistically significant positive effect on

Dealing with Student issues

cognitive and socioemotional outcomes from mindfulness practices in the schools but no significant effect on academic and behavioral outcomes. A third meta-analysis (Klingbeil et al., 2017), examining 76 studies involving 6,121 participants, found small positive effects (.32 in controlled studies), which surprisingly became stronger at follow-up (.46), suggesting that mindfulness has a cascading effect long after the study has ended.

Taken as a whole, these studies suggest small to moderate positive effects due to mindfulness-based practices in the schools. We must keep in mind, however, that the research on mindfulness in education is still in its infancy, and future studies will help to illuminate which factors are most potent in initiating positive effects on students' emotional well-being, cognitive performance, and academic achievement. Future studies also promise to indicate which interventions are most effective with specific groups of students.

Teacher and Student Testimonials for Mindfulness

Another way to gain insight into the benefits of mindfulness in schools is to listen to the teachers who are implementing these practices. Laura Markus, 6th and 7th grade math teacher at Dunn Middle School in Los Olivos, California, reports that the school schedule "can be chaotic for some students. They often come to my classroom after science class, where they may still be excited from setting something on fire just minutes before. . . . Taking a few minutes for quiet meditation at the beginning of each class serves as a transition for students to get into a different mindset for learning the logic of math" (Dunn School, 2018). Jana Standish, school counselor at Colrain Central School in Colrain, Massachusetts, who leads mindfulness sessions for elementary school students, comments, "Children have so many activities—things they're expected to learn and memorize. They're taking in so much information . . . just taking a little time to pause and feel your breathing is helpful" (Broncaccio, 2018). Intervention teacher Stacey Achterhoff, who has worked with K–5 homeless students in the Duluth Public Schools in Minnesota, says,

There were just so many layers of yuck to get through before we could get to academics. . . . If we don't address the trauma, then the kids are going to become stunted in academic growth. . . . When I go into the classroom, I see that quiet magic of kids being able to settle into their own bodies. . . . They see there's power in being able to control what they can, when there are so many other things out of their control. (Zalaznick, 2017)

We can also learn from the students themselves about the impact that classroom-based mindfulness has had on their lives. One high school student who had participated in a mindful self-compassion program for adolescents said this:

Mindfulness has helped me focus because every day, I have like 20 pages to read in APUSH and APES [AP U.S. History and AP Environmental Science], and somehow right now it is hard to get reading, and every day I would come home and think "I don't want to do this," and so I wouldn't, but if I sat down and focused only on this and nothing else then I got it done and it didn't even take that long. So I actually like meditating and . . . focusing on my breath, because it helped me focus on my schoolwork. (Bluth, Gaylord, Campo, Mullarkey, & Hobbs, 2016, p. 485)

Another high school student involved in a mindfulness study of an alternative high school program reported, "When we started meditation, it seemed that I would get angry and stay angry, but now it seems when I get angry, I calm down quicker" (Wisner, 2014, p. 632). In Baltimore, Maryland, Patterson High School student Chris Bowman commented on the effect mindfulness has had on him personally:

Growing up without a father and stuff like that, I struggled with a lot of depression, a lot of grief, and a lot of just really bad—really bad zones of like suicidal thoughts. But I had to find a way to get out of that. A mindful moment is when you—you just take a deep breath in a moment of conflict and just—maybe you just look at that and just like, I can do this in a different way. I don't have to fight this person. I don't have to look [to] violence as the answer. (*PBS NewsHour*, 2017)

How Mindfulness Fits Within Existing Education Programs

Some teachers may think of mindfulness as just another program they have to squeeze into an already overcrowded school day. Rather than reducing stress, they believe, this extra "burden" added to their teaching load will only make them feel more stressed. Lynley Schroering, principal of Luhr Elementary in Louisville, Kentucky, responds to this concern by commenting, "Sometimes we feel like we don't have time to deal with all of those kinds of emotional issues with kids, but if we don't deal with those and build those relationships and have kids feel safe, they really can't learn. If kids don't feel safe and supported, then no learning is going to take place" (Wagner, 2018). "A teacher may think, I can't add another thing to my day . . . ," says Amy Saltzman, director of the Association for Mindfulness in Education, "[b]ut what teachers find is, if they start class with five minutes of mindfulness—movement, breathing, journaling—most teachers will report ending up with more teachable time" (Zalaznick, 2017).

Another reason mindfulness practices don't constitute an add-on component to the school day is that they can be easily integrated into programs and initiatives that teachers are already using in their classrooms (see Figure 1.1, p. 17). Mindfulness aligns well, for example, with the ASCD/CDC Whole School, Whole Community, Whole Child framework (Giles, Hunt, Lewallen, Potts-Datema, & Slade, 2014). Mindfulness represents a key tool in the establishment of a positive social and emotional climate in school; can be used as part of the counseling, psychological, and social services of a school; and can be integrated into the health education courses in a district; and mindful stretching activities can be integrated into the physical education and physical activity component of the ASCD/CDC model. In addition, mindfulness practices can be extended to school employees, families, and the broader community (see Chapter 8 for examples of the implementation of each of these components).

Mindfulness also aligns well with the framework of Social and Emotional Learning (SEL). The Collaborative for Academic, Social, and Emotional Learning (CASEL) lists five core competencies to be developed in SEL programs: (1) self-awareness, (2) self-management, (3) social awareness, (4) relationship skills, and (5) responsible decision making (CASEL, 2012). Mindfulness is directly related to the first two competencies. As students become more aware of their thoughts, feelings, perceptions, and sensations through mindfulness practice, they increase their own self-awareness. Similarly, by using mindfulness strategies to cope with strong emotions (e.g., by seeing them in perspective), students will improve their self-management skills. Mindfulness is also indirectly related to the other three core competencies. If we add kindness and compassion toward others as a key element in mindfulness practice (see Chapter 5), then students will be developing their social awareness (consideration of others' experiences) and improving their relationship skills. Finally, it seems clear that mindfulness also promotes responsible decision making, because students are apt to make better decisions if they are able to reduce stress, improve self-regulation, and maintain detachment from stressful situations. (For more on the connections between mindfulness and SEL, see Dorman, 2015; Lantieri & Zakrzewski, 2015).

Mindfulness practices can also be considered part of the tool kit for all three tiers of Positive Behavioral Interventions and Supports (PBIS). As a Tier 1 intervention, mindfulness-based programs serve as a classwide, schoolwide effort to promote problem prevention and wellness. Most of the mindfulness programs that are currently being implemented are applied in this "all students" way. At the targeted level (Tier 2), mindfulness has shown promise in working with small groups of students, including those at risk of having behavioral problems (see, for example, Wisner, 2014). Finally, at the individual Tier 3 level, interventions such as Mindfulness-Based Cognitive Therapy for Children (MBCT-C), which was developed for anxious or depressed children, might be delivered one-on-one through counseling and psychological services at the school or through allied health services (see Semple & Lee, 2014).

Finally, mindfulness works as a key element within the Universal Design for Learning (UDL) framework (Rose & Meyer, 2002). In the most current version of the Universal Design for Learning Guidelines (CAST, 2018), under "Provide Multiple Means of Engagement," is the

Figure 1.1

**How Mindfulness Aligns with
Existing Education Initiatives and Programs**

Educational Initiative or Program	Initiative or Program Elements That Align with Mindfulness Practices
ASCD/Centers for Disease Control (CDC) Whole School, Whole Community, Whole Child Model (WSCC)	— Social and Emotional Climate — Counseling, Psychological, and Social Services — Health Education — Physical Education and Physical Activity
Social and Emotional Learning (SEL) programs	Core competencies: — Self-awareness — Self-management
Positive Behavioral Interventions and Supports (PBIS)	— Tier 1—Delivery to whole-class, whole-school populations as problem prevention and wellness promotion — Tier 2—Delivery to small groups at risk of behavioral problems — Tier 3—Delivery to individual students as therapy through psychological services
Universal Design for Learning (UDL)	Provide Multiple Means of Engagement — 9—Provide Options for Self-Regulation - 9.2—Facilitate personal coping skills and strategies Provide Multiple Means of Action and Expression — 4—Provide Options for Executive Functions

subheading "Provide Options for Self-Regulation." As we've seen in the research already cited, mindfulness functions as an effective strategy for self-regulation. UDL guideline 9.2 applies particularly well: "Facilitate personal coping skills and strategies." By teaching students mindfulness skills, we're empowering them with practical ways of reducing stress, managing strong emotions, improving attention span, and strengthening working memory. Mindfulness also appears to support the guideline relating to "Provide Multiple Means of Action and Expression" and its subheading "Provide options for Executive Functions." As noted, mindfulness has been shown to be effective in improving executive functioning and thus promotes each of the options described under this subheading (goal setting, planning, managing information, and monitoring progress).

The stakes for helping our students regulate their own emotions, thoughts, and behaviors have never been higher. In one highly influential study that tracked 1,000 children from birth to age 32, self-control ability predicted later physical health, substance dependence, personal finances, and criminal offense outcomes (Moffitt et al., 2011). These findings were independent of socioeconomic status, intelligence, and "mistakes" made in adolescence. In other words, failure to develop self-control is associated with higher costs to society through poorer physical and mental health, financial difficulties, and run-ins with the law. Teaching students mindfulness practices promises to make a significant contribution toward developing those self-control abilities in our children and adolescents that are vital for their own success and for the well-being of society as a whole. And these huge returns are possible with only a few minutes of daily classroom practice. How could one say no to such an opportunity!

Takeaways

- Stress levels in children and adolescents are at an all-time high, and much of this stress is school based.
- Mindfulness, or the intentional focus of awareness on the present moment, has been shown in thousands of studies with adults to have a significant positive impact on cognitive and emotional functioning.
- Mindfulness practices are increasingly being implemented in schools in the United States, the United Kingdom, and Australia.
- Mindfulness practices promise to relieve stress in students and bolster their self-regulation skills, working memory, executive functioning, and social and emotional development.

- Mindfulness aligns with existing programs, including the ASCD/CDC Whole School, Whole Community, Whole Child initiative; Social and Emotional Learning (SEL); Positive Behavioral Interventions and Supports (PBIS); and Universal Design for Learning (UDL).
- By giving students self-control abilities through mindfulness practices, we can make a direct positive contribution to their future health outcomes, financial status, and social adjustment as adults.

2

Reviewing Evidence from Neuroscience

One of the most remarkable features of mindfulness practice is that it positively affects both functional and structural areas of key brain centers. Research shows that mindfulness is able to help individuals reduce stress, focus attention, improve working memory, and support a variety of executive functioning processes. In this chapter we'll look at some of the neuroscience findings that support mindfulness meditation as a potent agent for helping our students manage their schoolwork and their lives.

Perhaps the most important feature of mindfulness in the schools is its capacity to reduce stress. As noted in Chapter 1, our students are coping with increasing levels of stress in today's complex world. Stress in itself is not a bad thing. In fact, stress evolved as a way to protect the human species as it faced dangers from animal and human predators, inclement weather, and other unpredictable forces in the wild. An individual who faced a lion with a blasé attitude was quickly eaten and wasn't able to pass its genes on to future generations. However, an individual who was biologically primed to respond with alarm and mobilize her physiology to escape the lion was more likely to survive and contribute to human evolution.

The Brain and Stress

Through evolution, humans have developed two key stress-response systems as a way of dealing with threats from the outside world (see Figure 2.1). The first is the fight-or-flight response, also known as the *sympathomedullary pathway*, or SAM axis. When a human confronts a danger, the senses relay that threat to the *amygdala*, an almond-shaped structure in the limbic system or "emotional brain," which interprets the external stimuli as dangerous and sends a distress signal to the *hypothalamus*, another part of the limbic system. The hypothalamus activates the *sympathetic nervous system*, a series of interconnected neurons in the spinal cord and the peripheral nervous system. This then triggers the *adrenal medulla* (the inner part of the adrenal gland) to secrete two key hormones, *adrenaline* and *noradrenaline*, which activate a range of physiological processes including increased heart rate and respiration (delivering more oxygen to the blood), decreased digestion (diverting energy to areas of the body where they're urgently needed), and the release of glucose (a quick energy source) from the liver. These bodily changes are what the body needs to cope with acute stressors like a large animal or an attacking tribe: immediate access to the energy necessary for running from the threat or facing it and fight- ing it (or, alternatively, freezing and hoping the threat doesn't notice you and goes away).

The second important stress response in humans is the *hypothal- amus-pituitary-adrenal axis*, or HPA axis, which is our central stress- response system (except for the acute stressors taken up by the SAM axis). In this case, stress activates the *hypothalamus*, which releases *corticotropin releasing factor* (CRF), which in turn releases *adreno- corticotropic hormone* (ACTH) in the pituitary. This action stimulates the release of *glucocorticoids*, primarily *cortisol* (a hormone—CORT), in the adrenal glands. Unlike the SAM axis, which happens almost instantaneously, the HPA axis extends over a period of hours. Then, as the threat diminishes, cortisol exerts negative feedback to the other hormones, bringing the system back to *homeostasis*, a state of equi- librium or stability. If the threat doesn't diminish, however, HPA axis activity becomes chronic (a condition known as *allostatic load*), lead- ing to several negative effects on physical and mental health.

Figure 2.1

Short-Term and Long-Term Stress Response

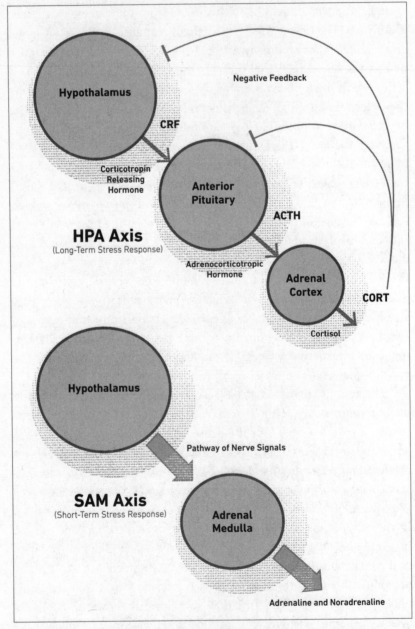

Source: HPA Axis Diagram adapted from https://commons.wikimedia.org/wiki/File:HPA_Axis_
Diagram_(Brian_M_Sweis_2012).png

This is what happens to many students. As mindfulness instructor Emma Reynolds (2018) puts it:

> It's in our genes to be on the alert for danger—our cavemen and cavewomen ancestors that didn't take notice of potential threats got eaten! . . . Fear is hard-wired into us as part of our survival kit, and the problem is we get triggered too easily by it in our busy lives. There are no tigers on the high street, but our caveman and cavewoman systems don't know that. The thoughts, emotions, and stress on the body and mind can be exhausting. Teachers are very much on the front line and can suffer from burnout all too easily. And students, with a more heightened sensitivity to stress, may find it more difficult to regulate their thoughts and emotions in the face of stressful life events such as exams. (p. 15)

This situation is particularly true of students who come to school from chronically stressful home environments. The Center on the Developing Child (2018) at Harvard University refers to this as "toxic stress." The center notes that this form of stress

> can occur when a child experiences strong, frequent, and/or pro-longed adversity—such as physical or emotional abuse, chronic neglect, caregiver substance abuse or mental illness, exposure to vio-lence, and/or the accumulated burdens of family economic hardship —without adequate adult support. This kind of prolonged activation of the stress response systems can disrupt the development of brain architecture and other organic systems, and increase the risk for stress-related disease and cognitive impairment well into the adult years.

As the mindfulness training center Mindfulschools.org (2018) puts it, "When a 4th grader reports that she felt she 'was going to die' from test anxiety, she's telling the truth. The responses of her autonomic nervous system are the same whether she's taking a math test or sensing actual physical danger."

How Mindfulness Teaches the Brain to De-Stress

Neuroscience research suggests that mindfulness alters the stress-producing pathways of the brain in three different ways. First, it appears to recruit stress-regulating areas of the prefrontal cortex (see Figure 2.2), including the ventral and dorsal regions, in inhibiting activity in stress-producing regions of the brain, following a kind of "top-down" regulatory pathway (Creswell & Lindsay, 2014). A highly simplified way of restating this would be that the "rational brain" is able to "talk some sense" into the "emotional brain." The prefrontal cortex is where the executive functions of the brain are located, including the ability to reflect, plan, organize, and self-regulate. These rational areas of the brain are able to resolve affective conflicts through executive processes such as abstract reasoning, planning, working memory, and reflection.

Figure 2.2

The Prefrontal Cortex

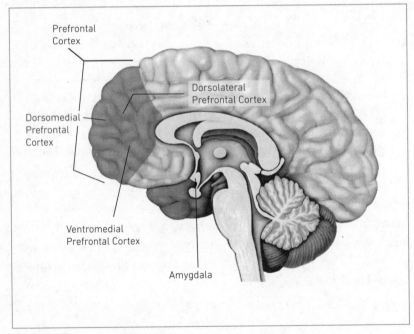

Source: NIH Medical Arts. Adapted from https://openi.nlm.nih.gov/detailedresult?img= PMC4623976_pbio.1002283.g001&req=4

One example of how this works in the laboratory is through the use of the "Stroop task," which presents subjects with colored cards upon which the names of conflicting colors are written (e.g., a blue card with the name "green" inscribed on it). Subjects who had been through brief mindfulness training demonstrated greater ability than subjects in a control group to resolve the affective conflict between word and color, and they displayed greater prefrontal cortex response as measured by functional MRI (Allen et al., 2012). Research suggests that inexperienced meditators are more likely to display this "top-down" approach, in which executive functions in the prefrontal cortex essentially buffer stress-producing regions of the brain such as the amygdala (Taylor et al., 2011).

A second way in which mindfulness practice appears to reduce stress is by directly affecting the stress-producing regions themselves (a "bottom-up" regulatory pathway). One finding, for example, is that mindfulness alters amygdala function by reducing its resting-state activity (Taren et al., 2015). As noted previously, the amygdala is a key brain region for detecting danger or threat and initiating a cascade of stress-related responses throughout the nervous system, the circulatory system, and the respiratory system. Thus, reducing the activation of the amygdala is a direct way of intervening in chronic stress. Even more remarkably, mindfulness training appears to change the structure of the amygdala, reducing its gray matter density (Hölzel et al., 2010; Hölzel et al., 2011). Research suggests that experienced practitioners of mindfulness are more likely to display this "bottom-up" regulatory strategy (Taylor et al., 2011).

Finally, a third way that mindfulness can promote stress reduction on a physiological level is through activation of the *parasympathetic nervous system*, which is a network that is complementary to the *sympathetic nervous system* and that can reduce the stress-related effects of the sympathetic nervous system (see Figure 2.3). The parasympathetic nervous system works to conserve energy by slowing down the heart rate, increasing digestive and glandular activity, and relaxing sphincter muscles in the gastrointestinal tract (it is also called the "rest-and-digest" system). This system evolved in humans as a way of adapting to nonstressful situations, when conditions were ripe for feeding and breeding. Research has suggested that mindfulness practices may

Figure 2.3

The Parasympathetic and Sympathetic Nervous Systems

Parasympathetic Nervous System	Sympathetic Nervous System
Constricts pupils	Dilates pupils
Stimulates salivation	Inhibits salivation
Slows heart rate	Increases heart rate
Constricts bronchi	Inhibits digestion
Stimulates digestion	Inhibits contraction of bladder
Causes bladder to contract	

increase parasympathetic nervous system activation indicators such as lowered blood pressure (Ditto, Eclache, & Goldman, 2006).

How Mindfulness Changes the Brain

Several other brain regions are functionally or structurally changed by mindfulness training. One is the *hippocampus*, a seahorse-shaped structure located inside the temple on each side of the brain in the limbic system (see Figure 2.4). It is involved in learning and memory processes and in the modulation of emotional control. It can be damaged by chronic stress (people with PTSD and depression tend to have smaller hippocampi). The density of gray matter in the hippocampus increases after mindfulness training (Luders, Toga, Lepore, & Gaser, 2009). Another area that changes in response to mindfulness is the *insula* (see Figure 2.5), a region of the brain buried deep in the cerebral cortex that is involved in awareness (consciousness) and in regulation of the body's homeostasis. It is particularly important in *interoception* (the sensation of inner bodily states such as hunger, breathing, or muscle tension). Mindfulness-based training increases the volume of a practitioner's insula (Lazar et al., 2005). Researchers have also noted mindfulness-related changes in gray-matter density of several other brain regions involved in regulation of emotion, self-referential processing, and perspective taking, including the posterior cingulate gyrus and the cerebellum (Hölzel et al., 2011).

Figure 2.4

The Limbic System

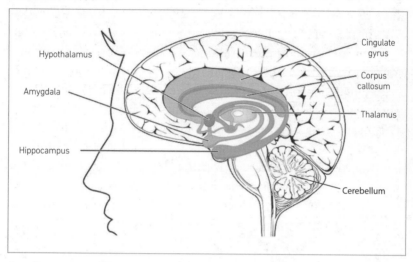

Source: Image from *Anatomy and Physiology* by OpenStax is licensed under CC BY 4.0.

Figure 2.5

The Insula of the Human Brain

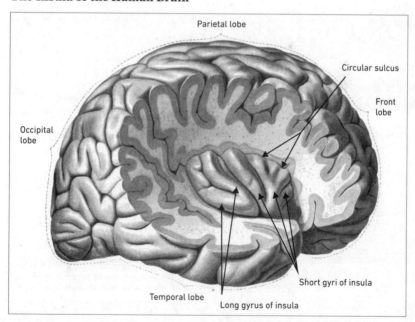

Source: An anatomical illustration from the 1908 edition of Sobotta's *Anatomy Atlas.*

A look at individual brain regions gives us only a partial understanding of how the brain changes as a result of mindfulness training. More recent research emphasizes the *functional connectivity* that exists in areas of the brain that are spatially separated from each other. So, for example, mindfulness training reduces resting-state functional connectivity of the right amygdala and *subgenual anterior cingulate cortex* (an area involved in negative affect states such as sadness and depression). This suggests that mindfulness may reduce the strength of connectivity of brain networks that drive stress reactivity (Taren et al., 2015). Other research suggests that mindfulness-based stress reduction results in increased functional connectivity between the auditory cortex and areas of the brain associated with attentional and self-referential processes, which in turn suggests a greater reflective awareness of sensory processes (Kilpatrick et al., 2011).

Mind Wandering and the Default Mode Network

Perhaps the most interesting brain network involved in mindfulness practice is the *default mode network,* or DMN (see Figure 2.6). This large-scale network of interacting brain regions includes the *angular gyrus* (located in the parietal lobe), the *medial prefrontal cortex*, the *posterior cingulate cortex* (the upper part of the limbic lobe), and the *precuneus* (located in the parietal lobe). The default mode network is associated with mind wandering, daydreaming, planning for the future, remembering the past, and constructing stories about the self. It activates when the brain is not specifically involved in a task (hence, it is the "default" state).

Research suggests that our minds wander a lot—in one study, 46.9 percent of the time (Killingsworth & Gilbert, 2010). Clearly, mind wandering is a formidable obstacle in the classroom, where a student's daydreaming can interfere with the comprehension of the lesson being presented. As it turns out, people who are experienced in mindfulness practices have *weaker* functional connectivity between DMN regions associated with self-referential processing and emotional appraisal and *stronger* connectivity between other DMN regions, suggesting strengthened awareness of the present moment (Taylor et al., 2013). In

Figure 2.6

The Default Mode Network

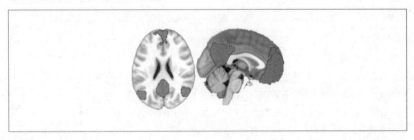

Source: Illustration © 2014 Baliki et al. This is part of an image that appears in Baliki, M. N., Mansour, A. R., Baria, A. T., & Apkarian, A. V. (2014). Functional Reorganization of the Default Mode Network across Chronic Pain Conditions. PLoS ONE 9(9): e106133. https://doi.org/10.1371/journal.pone.0106133

one study of college students, subjects who had practiced mindfulness had less mind wandering, better working memory, and a 16-percentile-point increase on the Graduate Record Exam (GRE) compared with a control group (Mrazek, Franklin, Phillips, Baird, & Schooler, 2013).

The upshot of all this research is that mindfulness practices appear to have a profound effect on the brain. Particularly remarkable is the way in which mindfulness initiates neuroplastic changes in the brain. Most of the research mentioned here was conducted with adults, who have limited neuroplasticity compared with younger individuals. The brains of children and teenagers are still developing and possess a much higher degree of neuroplasticity (Kolb & Gibb, 2011). Consequently, the neuroplastic changes noted in this research are likely to be even greater with younger individuals and to have a longer-lasting effect on their lives. We must keep in mind that the stress-response systems of children and teens are still developing, and, as we've seen, they can be damaged by chronic stress. Mindfulness practice provides a means of intervening at a critical stage in students' development and equipping them with the tools they need to face the inevitable stresses that life presents to them.

Takeaways

• Although the stress response is a normal physiological reaction that evolved to help humans cope with extreme events (e.g., predators, war, cataclysms), prolonged exposure to stressful events can have a debilitating effect on both mental and physical health. This is especially true for students growing up in impoverished urban areas, where toxic stress can lead to an increased risk for stress-related disease and cognitive impairment well into the adult years.

• There are two key stress-response systems: the SAM axis, which mobilizes the sympathetic nervous system to produce the hormones adrenalin and noradrenalin that stimulate the body to take quick action; and the HPA axis, a slower stress-response system that signals the adrenal glands to secrete the stress hormone cortisol to monitor and respond to stressful events.

• Mindfulness practices alter the stress-producing pathways of the brain in three ways: by activating executive functions in the prefrontal cortex (e.g., emotional self-regulation, reflection, planning) to buffer against limbic system reactivity ("top-down" regulation), by reducing the reactivity of stress-producing regions such as the amygdala ("bottom-up" regulation), and by directly decreasing activity in the sympathetic nervous system (e.g., by lowering blood pressure) and activating the parasympathetic nervous system.

• Mindfulness practices appear to change functional and structural regions in the brain including the amygdala (which signals threatening events to the brain), the hippocampus (important in learning and memory), and the insula (important for monitoring somatic experiences such as hunger or thirst).

• Brain research is increasingly focused not just on activity in single areas of the brain but on functional connectivity between spatially distant regions. Of particular importance is the default mode network (a system associated with mind wandering), which appears to be significantly altered by mindfulness practices.

3

Understanding the Basics

The essence of mindfulness is simple: by attending to the present moment with an attitude of acceptance, openness, and curiosity, we can train our minds, regulate our emotions, control our behaviors, and cultivate healthier relationships with the people and events around us. This process has three components. The first is *focus.* This could be a focus on our breathing, our bodily sensations, our eating, our walking, or any other tangible activity that we're engaged in during the course of a day. The second component is *open monitoring,* which involves noticing our inner and outer experiences in whatever form they happen to take, as they arise from moment to moment within our awareness. The third component is *attitude,* and in particular, having an open, non-judgmental, curious attitude toward whatever experience comes up as we practice.

The Simple Magic of Breathing

The most common form of mindfulness practice involves sitting and focusing on one's breathing (see Figure 3.1). Making the breath the focus of mindfulness is quite handy because as long as we're alive, we're always breathing, and we take our breathing with us wherever we go. Pay attention to your own breathing for a moment. It helps to focus on the physical sensations of breathing. Some people like to focus on the rise and fall of the belly with every inhale and exhale. Others prefer to focus on the air rushing into their nostrils on the inhale (giving a cool sensation) and the air exiting their nostrils on the exhale (giving a warm sensation). To help with focus, some people like to count each breath from 1 to 10 and then start over, or to say the words *in* on the inhale and *out* on the exhale. The important thing is that our breath is the core event of this practice to which we're always returning whenever we get distracted.

And distracted we are sure to be. I've been practicing mindful breathing for 30 years, and despite my best efforts to focus (I usually sit for 30 minutes at a time), my mind wanders umpteen times during a session. As noted in Chapter 2, one study suggests that our minds wander almost half our waking hours (Killingsworth & Gilbert, 2010). This wandering is normal. The fact that our minds are so restless is a *given* in mindfulness practice and is important to the process because it creates the opportunity for nonjudgmental monitoring of experiences. These may include emotions ("I'm getting bored"), thoughts ("I've got a test next period"), perceptions (the sounds of birds outside), or sensations (the itch on the tip of my nose). In each case, whatever it happens to be, we simply notice the experience in a nonjudgmental, curious way and then return our attention to our breathing. Some people find it useful to label the distractions ("boring," "planning," "hearing," or "itching") before returning their focus on their breath. If we could transcribe the process in the mind of a 12th grade boy during a typical mindfulness session, it might look something like this:

> *in... out... in... out... I'm not sure I'm doing it right...judging... in ... out... in... What's that noise?... hearing air conditioner... in... out... in... out... Oh no! I forgot to hand in that assignment that was due today!... remembering... in... out... in... out... I'm so mad at my brother for hogging the computer last night... anger... in... out ... in... out... I've got to get my sister a birthday present...planning ... in... out... in... What if that hot new girl in class started to pay attention to me?... imagining... in... out... in... out... in... out... This is boring...feeling bored... in... out... in... out... in... out...*

Figure 3.1
Mindful Breathing

Note: This is not a script to be read aloud to students; rather, it is a framework to use in leading students in a session of mindful breathing. The length, the pacing, and the nature of the teacher prompts to be used during the session are determined by teachers according to the level and needs of their students.

— Ask students to sit in a chair with feet flat on the floor and in an upright posture, hands folded in the lap or placed on the knees (or on a table or desk), and eyes closed. (Note: The practice can also be done lying down; however, this may not be the best arrangement for those who are apt to fall asleep. Also, some students may prefer keeping their eyes open and they can look at the floor or at some fixed spot in the classroom.)

— Use the timer on your smartphone to set the time you plan to practice (for example, from one minute to half an hour). Pick a starting and ending tone or signal that is pleasant to hear. Alternatively, designate someone to ring a bell to start and end each session.

— At the starting tone, ask students to become aware of their normal respiration. Suggest that they pay attention to each inhalation and exhalation. Tell them that if it helps, they may silently say "in" on the inhalation and "out" on the exhalation, or count each breath from 1 to 10 and then start over (they may count on their fingers as they do this). Also, suggest that they pick an area to focus on as they breathe: the rising and falling of the belly or chest, or the cool inrush of air in the nostrils on the inhalation and the warm outgo of air on the exhalation.

— Have them continue breathing, not trying to control the breath in any way, simply breathing normally.

— After a minute or so, tell students that if they become distracted at any time by a thought (such as a memory), a feeling (such as boredom), a sensation (such as pain in the knee), or a perception (such as noise outside) to simply notice it without judgment and then return to their breathing.

— At intervals (every few minutes) remind students to stay focused on their breathing, and whenever they are interrupted by any stimulus in their mind or in the outside environment, ask them to observe it for a moment, perhaps label it (for example, "noise," "joy," "ache," "memory," "planning"), and then return to their breathing.

— Repeat this process until the tone or signal indicates the end of session.

Remember (and remind students), there is no wrong way to do this, and it is not a competition to see who can do it better.

Not Getting Tangled Up in Our Stories

This process of noticing what distracts us in a nonjudgmental way is key to mindfulness practice. Instead of getting caught up in the experience of, let's say, "anger" and stewing in our juices or acting out the feeling toward the person or experience perceived to have caused it (e.g., through an insult or a fight), the anger is simply noticed, labeled, and let go of as the individual returns to the breathing.

One of the phrases I really like in the mindfulness movement is "thoughts are not facts." In other words, the anger that just came up for me is not a reality that I have to react to but a feeling that arises and falls away. Another helpful concept is the idea that when our mind wanders, we often tell ourselves "stories." For example, I might experience feelings of anxiety toward a bully in school. In my mind I might spin a story to exacerbate this fear ("I'm always getting bullied . . . What's wrong with me . . . I'm a walking target . . ."). In mindfulness, we simply observe the experience of fear or thoughts about the bully and leave the story behind without getting tangled up in it (which isn't to say that the problem of bullying shouldn't be handled in some proactive way later on). This kind of discovery offers a real liberation. Ben Belnap, associate superintendent of student wellness in the Park City School District in Park City, Utah, says,

> [Mindfulness] helps us to not just be pinballs being bounced around from one thing to another, reacting to this and reacting to that. It helps us to stop . . . and look at our thoughts and say "I'm feeling angry right now. Why am I feeling angry? What does being angry feel like inside physically?" Just sort of pump the brakes. (King, 2017)

It's useful to focus on *normal* breathing during mindfulness practice. Taking deep breaths can be helpful in situations where we want to de-stress quickly (e.g., before a test, during a stressful interaction with someone), when we're doing certain mindful stretching poses, or otherwise seek a state of deep relaxation. Normal breathing, however, and the awareness of it from moment to moment, provides all that we really need to engage in a mindfulness practice. Some mindfulness educators have implemented special breathing exercises such as alternate breathing through right and left nostrils, fire breathing (quick deep breaths), and other techniques, but these practices can result in adverse consequences such as hyperventilation, faintness, dizziness, or in rare cases the potential for releasing powerful memories and emotions. Moreover, these exercises are linked to yogic practices and risk crossing the line separating church and state in public schools in the United States.

Healthy normal breathing begins in the belly, where inhalation pulls the diaphragm (a strong sheet of muscle that divides the chest from the abdomen) downward, allowing the lungs more space to fill up with oxygen. Chest breathing, by contrast, doesn't engage the diaphragm in this way and thus results in a shallower breath, delivering less oxygen to the blood stream. One technique that the Center for Healthy Minds at the University of Wisconsin has developed to teach kindergartners "belly breathing" is to lie down on a mat and put a "belly buddy"—a stuffed animal or a stone, for example—on their abdomen, where they can watch it rise and fall during normal respiration.

A common myth about mindfulness is that it will make kids more relaxed. Although this might be true of deep-breathing exercises, the actual practice of mindful breathing is not intended to make the person more relaxed. Rather, it's intended to help the individual develop a greater awareness of moment-to-moment experience. This process of focusing on the breath noticing distractions without judgment, and then returning to the breath helps train the mind to process life experiences with a certain degree of detachment, so that we aren't derailed by the flux and flow of either subjective or objective occurrences. It helps students become aware of how much time they spend worrying about past events, fretting about the future, getting thrown out of joint by strong emotions, or becoming distracted by errant thoughts. The process of continually returning to one's breath actually trains the "attention muscles" in the brain so that they get stronger. It also expands the capacity of the mind to observe its own thinking processes (which is why research on mindfulness shows executive functions becoming stronger).

I've been referring to mindfulness as a *practice,* and that's exactly what it is. By practicing focused attention, open monitoring of experience, and a nonjudgmental attitude concerning whatever comes up, students get better at these functions, just as if they were practicing a musical instrument or learning a foreign language.

Mindfulness is also a process that has no fixed outcome beyond the start and stop time of each period of practice. This type of activity runs counter to the objectives of most school projects, courses, or endeavors, where there are specific outcomes. Mindfulness involves no grades, no test results, no final report on how good a meditator you've been, no bulletin board where the abilities of students as meditators are ranked (and if any of these things are being done in the classroom, they represent faulty implementations that should be stopped immediately; see Chapter 10). But mindfulness *does* lead to results that educators can see over time: better self-regulation, more concentrated attention, more positive self-regard, a kinder attitude toward classmates, and more successful experiences in school and life. As one Bronx high school student, who struggled with painful emotions and would often cry in class, said after practicing mindfulness, "I noticed that I could feel [my breath] in my chest. . . . And at that moment, I felt so relieved. The only thing I could think in my mind was, 'I'm OK.' And, I don't know—from that day on, it just didn't hurt anymore" (Davis, 2015).

Formal Versus Informal Mindfulness Practices

One important distinction to make with regard to mindfulness practices is between *formal* practices and *informal* practices. Formal practices are those experiences of mindfulness that are deliberate, time limited, and have a specific focus. Earlier I described one of those formal practices, *mindful breathing*. There are other types of formal practice. There's *mindful walking* (Figure 3.2), in which the focus is on the steps one takes during a deliberate walk up and down a defined pathway (or in a circle). Instead of paying attention to the breath, here the person focuses on the feelings of contact that the feet make on the ground, the experience of the legs rising and falling, and other bodily sensations attendant to walking. As with mindful breathing, distractions are bound to occur, and the instructions are the same: to notice the distractions without judgment and return to the sensations of walking. There is also *mindful eating* (Figure 3.3), which focuses on the sensations of eating—the smell, taste, and texture of the food and the experience of chewing and swallowing.

Another practice that has been developed as part of the Mindfulness-Based Stress Reduction program spearheaded by Jon

Figure 3.2

Mindful Walking

For highly active kids, and also for a change in the routine of mindful breathing, students can do mindful walking.

— Prearrange a path for walking. In the classroom, you can have the students walk in a circle around the perimeter of the room. Outside—on the playground, for example—you might designate a straight path to and from various locations. In nature, where there are abundant paths, a freestyle form of walking may be more suitable.

— Before your students begin walking, ask them to be mindful of their whole body, and in particular, of the contact that their feet make with the ground. Then ask them to slowly take the first step, focusing on the rising and falling of the leg and foot. They might experience the heel contacting the ground first, followed by the sole and the toes. Then, still slowly, students take the next step and then the one after that, so that as they walk they are concentrating on each foot's connection to the ground, the alternate raising and falling of their legs, the contractions in their leg muscles as they move along, the sensation of their arms swinging back and forth, and the experience of their whole body moving through space.

— If students are walking in nature, it may also be appropriate to focus on natural elements such as the gusting of wind, the calling of birds, the rushing of water, the scurrying of animals, and the beaming of sunlight on the trees and landscape. As with the other mindfulness practices, if the mind becomes distracted by thoughts, feelings, or other extraneous stimuli, simply notice the distraction in a nonjudgmental way and return the focus to the sensations of walking.

Figure 3.3

Mindful Eating

To do this exercise, you will need a raisin (or substitute a grape, a small piece of candy, or a slice of an apple or orange). Guide the students through the following steps, pausing after each one to give them time for the experience.

— Hold the raisin between two fingers or in your hand and then
  - look at its shape;
  - observe its wrinkles;
  - feel its texture;
  - smell it; and
  - notice any feelings of anticipation, salivation, hunger, or other sensations in your mouth.

— Very gently place the raisin in your mouth, but don't eat it right away. Instead,
  - feel the textures of the raisin on your tongue
  - notice any taste coming from the whole raisin in your mouth.

continued

Figure 3.3 (continued)
Mindful Eating

— Slowly bite into the raisin (but don't swallow it yet) and
  - feel the sensations of biting into the raisin (in your teeth, jaw, lips);
  - notice any flavors it releases;
  - feel the coming apart of the raisin in your mouth and the sensations of the raisin pieces in different parts of your mouth; and
  - notice any salivation as you chew.
— Observe the desire to want to swallow the raisin, but hold off until you've fully experienced the pieces of raisin in your mouth, the flavors, the textures, the smells.
— Slowly swallow the raisin and
  - notice the muscles in your mouth and throat as they expand or contract while swallowing;
  - feel the raisin pieces going down your throat; and
  - see if you can tell how far down the raisin pieces go before you no longer feel them in your body.
— After you've swallowed,
  - observe the aftertaste of the raisin in your mouth;
  - notice any remaining bits of raisin that are still in your mouth or on your teeth;
  - notice your tongue as it licks your lips and travels around in your mouth looking for any remaining bits of raisin; and
  - notice your swallowing of these remaining pieces.
  - Stay present with your body for a few moments after eating the raisin, feeling any sensations in your mouth, throat, or stomach from having eaten it.

Kabat-Zinn (2013) is called *body scan* (Figure 3.4). This practice is usually done while lying down (though it can be done sitting in a chair) and involves becoming aware of different sensations in the body, progressively working from the feet to the head. Finally, there's *mindful stretching* (Figure 3.5), in which the individual focuses on the specific pose and the sensations involved in moving into a pose or changing from one pose to another.

Figure 3.4
Body Scan

This practice is best done lying down, although it also can be experienced while in a sitting or reclining position.
— Ask students to become aware of their whole body and of the contact that their body makes with the floor (if lying down) or the chair (if seated). Also ask them to initially become aware of their breathing (although breathing will not be the focus of this practice).

— Starting with the feet and toes, ask students to become aware of sensations in each part of the body (for example, "now focus your attention on your toes"). Follow this progression in focusing awareness:

– toes	– stomach	– elbows
– feet	– chest	– upper arms
– ankles	– lower back	– shoulders
– lower legs and calves	– upper back	– neck
– upper legs and thighs	– fingers	– face
– pelvis	– lower arms	– scalp

— Depending upon the time available, spend a few moments or longer lingering at each point in the body scan, feeling whatever sensations (or lack of sensations) are present in that part of the body, including tingling, aching, sweating, itching, shaking, pulsing, pain, pleasure, tickling, warmth, coolness, fatigue, heaviness, lightness, energy, anxiety, rumbling, hunger, fear, relaxation, thirst, shivering, numbness, or nausea.

There's nothing that the individual needs to do other than experience as fully as possible whatever is going on in each part of the body. As with the other practices, if distractions or mind wandering occur, simply notice nonjudgmentally and then return to the focus on each designated part of the body.

Figure 3.5

Mindful Stretching

Mindful stretching is sometimes equated with yoga, but the two are very different in many ways. Yoga is an ancient Hindu tradition, with many different kinds of practices. Hatha yoga is the form most closely related to the body, but there are many esoteric practices related to the postures that are not part of mindful stretching. Simply put, mindful stretching involves moving into different physical positions or postures and being totally present while doing so. Here are descriptions of three common poses:

— Mountain Pose—The simplest pose is sometimes called the Mountain Pose, which involves standing straight and tall with hands at your side and legs together with equal weight on each foot. It's a position of strength and can be used to move into other poses, such as the Tree Pose.

— Tree Pose—Starting from the Mountain Pose, lift one leg and place the bottom of the foot against the inner thigh of the other leg (doing so requires balance, which is easier if you focus on a stable point on a wall). Be especially careful not to press the foot against your knee joint as this can lead to joint problems. Then raise your hands above your head. Hold the pose for 15–30 seconds while concentrating your attention on your body and the feeling of being in that pose. Offer the option of putting one hand on the wall for stability.

continued

Figure 3.5 (continued)

Mindful Stretching

— Cobra Pose—Begin by lying face down and placing your hands (palms down) next to your shoulders. Then slowly raise your head and torso, like a cobra, while gently supporting your weight with your hands. To reduce strain on the back, let your pelvis take most of the weight. Hold the pose for 15–30 seconds while focusing on the bodily sensations of being in that position.

There are many other poses, and the best way to learn them is either directly from a teacher or by watching a video. For younger kids, a couple of good videos that teach some basic poses are "Kids Yoga with Sheila Palmquist" (https://www.youtube.com/watch?v=oWLSLpcF0iY) and "Yoga for Kids!" (https://youtube.com/watch?v=X655B4ISakg). For older students, try "Beginner Yoga for Kids and Teens Class" (https://www.youtube.com/watch?v=wsfJnS79GO8).

Informal practices, by contrast, are instances in which mindfulness is practiced in the midst of normal life experience: washing the dishes, cleaning the house (or classroom), showering, playing a sport, doing art, reading, completing a written assignment, riding a bike, driving a car, or nearly any other activity. We engage in many automatic activities every day, doing them without any focused concentration. The intention of informal mindfulness practice is to bring our awareness fully to whatever we happen to be doing. The advantage of informal practice is that it can be done anytime, anywhere. It's best if students have plenty of experience with formal practices first and then decide what they'd like to focus on as an informal practice. Educators might suggest as "home practice" that students pick something they do habitually—taking out the garbage, cleaning their room, building with blocks, even using technology—and practice focusing their whole attention on the activity, again treating distractions with a nonjudgmental, curious attitude.

Simple Ways to Get Started

Although mindful practice sessions can extend to 45 minutes or an hour for adult practitioners (and to multiday retreats where adults spend as many as 10 to 14 hours a day engaged in mindful practices), with children and adolescents you definitely want to start small. Research suggests that even 5- to 10-minute sessions can buffer negative affect and reduce impulsive behaviors (Britton et al., 2014; Creswell, 2017).

Perhaps the simplest way to begin is with a one-minute mindful listening session (simply being quiet and listening to the ambient sounds in and around the classroom: birds singing, people passing by in the hall, desks squeaking, the air vent humming, wind blowing leaves, people shifting in their seats). Another excellent introduction to mindfulness is a one-minute session that involves listening to a bell ring. Some educators ask students to raise their hands when they can no longer hear the bell. This bell activity is sometimes used as an entry point into a period of mindful sitting with a focus on the breath, and the bell is often used to signal the end of the session as well. Again, the recommendation is to start off with short periods of practice.

At Florence Griffith Joyner Elementary School in the Watts neighborhood of Los Angeles, teachers use a program called Calm Classroom, implemented by the UCLA Center for Child Anxiety, Resilience, and Support (CARES). The program leads students (transitional kindergartners through 5th graders) in three sessions of three-minute mindfulness practices over the course of a day. Principal Akida Kissane-Long notes that "[t]he children of Joyner Elementary have responded extremely well to the Calm Classroom training and practice.... Discipline referrals have admirably decreased in just three weeks of school" (Jupin, 2016). Limiting mindfulness practice to just two or three minutes at the start of a class means that it can be integrated into the classroom day without changing curricular timetables. It also provides a way for students to transition from their previous class or event (such as lunch or recess), which might have been highly active, into the new class with a calm disposition.

Practical Tips for Successful Mindfulness Programs

Here are some other practical tips for making mindful moments—whether for 1 minute or 30—count in your students' lives.

• ***Have students discuss their experiences after mindful practices.*** After engaging in mindful walking, 4th grade students at Ottawa Elementary School in Petoskey, Michigan, talked about everything from physical aches and pains to anxious emotions. They also shared experiences related to an earlier mindfulness session; one student mentioned having experienced a sense of joy, and another told of having experienced a moment of anger that he resolved by using a mindfulness strategy (Bassett, 2018).

Social and emotional learning strategies dovetail with mindfulness by teaching students the language of emotions and how they can be shared in a safe space. At Piedmont Avenue Elementary School in Oakland, California, one student began crying about her dead grandmother, while another sobbed about melted lip balm. Glenn Heyser, who teaches their combined 4th and 5th grade class, observed, "It tapped into a very emotional space for them. . . . They struggled with, 'Is it OK to go there?'" (Brown, 2007).

Sometimes it's necessary to ask for clarification on an experience, as when a teacher asked a group of kindergarten students how they felt after a mindfulness exercise and some of the children said "dead." A meditation teacher who was assisting the regular classroom teacher asked the children, "What does dead feel like?" and they answered, "like a swan," "like an angel," "like floating" (Saltzman & Goldin, 2008). Above all, it's important for students to know that sharing is optional and there is no expectation of any self-disclosure of personal information or content.

• *Consider the time and space for mindfulness.* When preparing the environment for mindful practices, make sure that you won't be interrupted. Place a sign on the door saying "Quiet please, we're practicing mindfulness" or something similar, and ask students to clear off their desks or get out their mats. Avoid circle seating, which can enable students to watch (and distract) each other, and select a regular time for mindfulness sessions, such as at the beginning or ending of a class period, before tests, or as "brain breaks." Make sure students have used the restroom before you begin, and pick a time when you know the school bell, announcements on the intercom, visitors, or other distractions won't interrupt the session.

• *Anticipate normal distractions.* Despite your best efforts, events are bound to intrude upon your mindfulness practices, so it's a good idea to plan ahead. If the custodian begins mowing the lawn outside the classroom, for example, simply weave the "interruption" into the mindfulness activity ("listen to the lawn mower . . . listening . . . now return to your breathing . . ."). Also, when you first start mindfulness practice with your class, it's normal to expect a certain amount of restlessness (or comments such as "this is boring") as students learn to adjust to the new routine. This reaction generally should dissipate as students become familiar with the practice of mindfulness. For students who are especially disruptive, have contingencies in place such as making an aide available to provide personalized assistance or referring students to a "mindful room" where they can receive one-on-one attention (see Chapter 8).

• *Use technology.* If you feel unprepared to lead mindfulness sessions with your students, you can use any one of a wide range of videos and audio apps with trained instructors leading listeners through various mindfulness practices. Video may be especially useful with mindful stretching, in which the movements and poses involve detailed sensory motor instructions. Appendix B provides a list of videos and smartphone apps.

• *Share your own experiences with mindfulness.* Chapter 4 makes a strong case for teachers taking up the practice of mindfulness themselves before or at the same time as their students. If you are doing this, it can be helpful to share stories of your own practice, for example, times when you used mindfulness to calm down during a period of stress, when it helped you handle a difficult emotion, or when it prompted you to act with kindness toward a difficult person. This sharing doesn't have to be (and really shouldn't be) a deeply personal soul-searching story, but a simple affirmation of the good that the practice is doing for you. Your students will be inspired by your example and take their practice more seriously.

• *Let students be involved in leading mindful practices.* It can be helpful for students' ownership of the mindfulness process if you involve them in the running of mindfulness activities. Set up a rotation schedule with students responsible for ringing the bell that begins and ends a mindfulness session. Let students lead the class in a round of mindful stretching exercises. They can also share what they've learned about mindfulness with students in the lower grades at their school.

• ***Don't use mindfulness practices as a substitute for classroom control.*** Mindfulness is a proactive self-regulation approach for students that should be entirely voluntary. If students don't wish to participate (or their parents don't want them to be involved), then allow them to sit or work quietly while the other students are practicing mindfulness. Also, avoid using mindfulness as a classroom management strategy. It's easy to fall into the trap of telling a disruptive student to "shape up and be mindful—or else!" There's sometimes a thin line between empowering students to internally engage in a mindful practice and trying to externally control behavior through subtly coercive messages ("Class! We're not being very mindful here!"). As mentioned in Chapter 4, if teachers have a mindfulness practice of their own, then they are able to deal with classroom behavioral issues coming from a place of calmness and detachment, which enables them to be more effective in helping students regain control from within.

In our achievement-conscious educational climate, students are apt to worry that they're "doing it all wrong" when it comes to mindfulness. Remember that mindfulness is a no-fail, self-paced practice. Students start wherever they are and proceed at their own rate. And in a sense, they're not really going anywhere at all. They're just practicing getting better at being in the "now," as mentioned in one of the cleverest titles of a mindfulness book: *Wherever You Go, There You Are* (Kabat-Zinn, 2005). Similarly, in our attention-deficit-disordered culture of fast-track technologies, it's likely that students (especially adolescents) will find some of the practices (especially mindful breathing) to be boring. In such cases, it makes more sense to switch to one of the more active practices such as mindful walking or mindful stretching. (Chapter 6 will explore how mindfulness practices can be adapted and adjusted for different grade levels.) Consider that it can be salutary for students to sit with their boredom from time to time, watching it and seeing if it changes into something else. Such a process may serve as a welcome antidote to the rapid pace of today's world.

Takeaways

- There are three key factors in any mindfulness practice: *focus* on an activity (such as breathing); *open monitoring* of ideas, feelings, and sensations that interrupt the focus; and a *nonjudgmental and curious attitude* toward whatever comes up.
- The most common type of formal mindfulness practice involves sitting and focusing on one's breathing, but other formal practices include mindful walking, mindful eating, body scan, and mindful stretching.
- In addition to formal mindfulness practices, there are informal practices that can include a wide range of normal human activities such as taking out the garbage, washing the dishes, cleaning the classroom, playing soccer, or getting dressed.
- Although mindfulness may make students feel more relaxed, this is not its chief function, which is to improve awareness of each present moment.
- Tips for implementing mindfulness in the classroom include the following: start small, provide opportunities to share experiences, use technology, prepare for potential interruptions, let students lead sessions, and avoid using mindfulness as a classroom management strategy.

4

Practicing Self-Care as a Teacher

Anyone who's flown a lot knows that the preflight announcements include directions for using oxygen masks if there should be a sudden loss of cabin pressure. Passengers are instructed to put on their own oxygen mask before helping anyone else (e.g., a child, an elderly person). The message is clear: if you don't put on your own oxygen mask and you pass out from lack of oxygen, then you won't be much good at helping anybody else. As much as you'd like to help another person, you need to think first about your own self-care. This metaphor illustrates the fact that before teachers introduce their students to mindfulness practices, they should establish a mindfulness practice of their own so that they have the alertness, level-headedness, and credibility to share what they know with their class.

The High Cost of Teacher Stress

There's a more immediate reason for teachers to begin practicing mindfulness before their students do: teachers are under enormous stress. In one study, 46 percent of teachers reported high daily stress during the school year, a figure that is tied with that of nurses for the highest stress rate of any occupational group in the United States (Gallup, 2014). Teachers ranked last in a survey of 12 occupational groups when it came to feeling that their opinions counted in the workplace. In the same survey, more than half of K–12 educators (56 percent) said they are "not engaged" in their work, meaning they are not connected emotionally with their work and are unlikely to devote much extra time to their teaching duties, while around 13 percent are "actively disengaged," meaning they are not satisfied with their workplace and are likely to spread negativity among their coworkers. The survey's authors conclude: "So if nearly 70% of teachers are just going through the motions at work—or worse, undermining student learning by spreading negativity—that's a big problem facing the nation's schools" (Gallup, 2014, p. 27).

The demands on teachers in today's 21st century learning environment are wide ranging. According to Patricia Jennings, associate professor of education in the Curry School of Education at the University of Virginia,

> [W]e ask an awful lot of teachers these days. . . . Beyond just conveying the course material, teachers are supposed to provide a nurturing learning environment, be responsive to students, parents and colleagues, juggle the demands of standardized testing, coach students through conflicts with peers, be exemplars of emotion regulation, handle disruptive behavior and generally be great role models; . . . the problem is we rarely give teachers training or resources for any of them. (Garrison Institute, 2009, p. 1)

And these are just the positive expectations. If a school lacks strong principal leadership, has an emotionally unhealthy school climate, or fails to nurture collegial relationships, then stress levels can become toxic. The Teacher Burnout Checklist in Figure 4.1 can help you determine if stress is a problem for you—a positive response to a single item may indicate that it is.

A stressed-out teacher is not an effective teacher. In a study of 121 teachers at elementary schools in a Midwestern school district, the teachers who reported the highest stress levels and lowest levels of coping also had the worst student outcomes, such as lower math scores and more disruptive behaviors (Herman, Hickmon-Rosa, & Reinke, 2017). A study conducted at the University of British Columbia

Figure 4.1
Teacher Burnout Checklist

Check any item that applies to you:

☐ I don't feel much support for what I do in the classroom from my school or district's leadership staff.

☐ I am afraid of being verbally or physically assaulted by students in my school.

☐ I feel so dispirited about my work, I sometimes feel like crying.

☐ I feel more and more pressure from administrators to teach to the test.

☐ I feel like I'm just told what to teach and not given much discretion or freedom in how I teach it.

☐ I feel that teachers at my school are at best unsupportive and at worst suspicious of or antagonistic toward my efforts to excel in teaching.

☐ I am spending increasing amounts of my valuable instructional time dealing with discipline issues in my classroom.

☐ I frequently get angry or upset at my students for not meeting my behavioral or academic expectations.

☐ I am given virtually no time at school to plan my lessons, consult with other teachers, or otherwise improve my teaching skills.

☐ I dread meeting with certain parents because of their demands or expectations of what they feel should take place in the classroom with regard to their kids.

☐ I worry about the mental health of certain students in my classroom and am concerned that nothing is being done to help them with their troubles.

☐ I take my worries home with me, and doing so can often interfere with my sleep or leisure-time activities.

tracked the levels of stress hormones in more than 400 elementary school students in 17 schools (grades 4 through 7). Researchers found that teachers who reported higher levels of burnout had students with the highest levels of the stress hormone cortisol every morning (Oberle & Schonert-Reichl, 2016). Another study reported in the *Journal of School Psychology* found that teachers with depressive symptoms spent less time in teacher-facilitated academic instruction provided to the whole class and less time in planning and organizing their instruction (McLean, Abry, Taylor, & Connor, 2018). A study of 1,001 Head Start teachers in Pennsylvania found that more workplace stress was associated with greater conflict in teacher-child relationships (Whitaker, Dearth-Wesley, & Gooze, 2015). Finally, an analysis of pooled data of 380 teachers and 7,899 4th grade students in Germany found that teachers' emotional exhaustion was negatively associated with students' grade point averages, results on standardized achievement tests, school satisfaction, and perceptions of teacher support (Arens & Morin, 2016).

We might modify a well-known proverb and say "Educator, heal thyself" as a way of emphasizing the importance of teachers learning self-care strategies that include mindfulness practices. Willem Kuyken, professor of clinical psychology at the University of Exeter in the U.K., observes, "It's become really clear that if you want to do this in schools, you have to start with teachers. . . . The teacher needs to embody the qualities [of mindfulness] they're trying to teach" (Lunau, 2014). Mindfulness teacher and researcher Karen Bluth concurs, "To truly understand what mindfulness entails, you have to do the practice and, in fact, embody that which the practice presents and teaches. [Otherwise, it] would be like teaching someone how to drive without ever having been behind a wheel" (New Harbinger Publications, 2015).

The Benefits of Teacher Mindfulness

Integrating mindfulness practices into the school day can work wonders for a teacher's mental and emotional health. One elementary school teacher in the Bronx reported,

> When administrators call you, you never know what they want. It could be a parent is upset with you, or you forgot something. . . . I used to rush to meetings, grab a seat, and jump in. Now, I practice mindful walking. I think about where I'm going. When I arrive, I'm not revved up. I'm able to receive criticism or conversation without being triggered. (Kamenetz, 2016)

Elementary school counselor Mandy Montgomery notes, "I have less anxiety and don't get as overwhelmed as quickly as I used to. . . . I am able to control my temper better and have an overall sense of peace most of the time" (Stevens, 2016). More important, mindfulness training provides teachers with a style of approaching students and student behavior that is calm and centered, not strained, reactive, or punitive. School counselor Christy Lynn Anana (2018) puts it this way:

As a school counselor, I help teachers understand the most important thing they can do for children is to keep their own mood stable. . . . Educators are in a unique position where we can role model keeping our body calm in the midst of a child's storm of dysregulation. By being present, we teach children resilience and build their capacity for enduring tough moments. We can also role model self-care. We can step back, ground ourselves in the moment, take a deep breath, and say within, "It's not about me."

Another way that mindfulness training can be helpful to educators is through its ability to reduce the occurrence of implicit biases that teachers may have of their students. One study, for example, demonstrated that by focusing on present-moment awareness, mindfulness practices help short-circuit automatically activated associations from previous experiences having to do with age and race (Lueke & Gibson, 2014). It is likely that mindfulness would also be helpful in reducing biases related to other differences, including disability status, gender identity, and socioeconomic level of students. Regarding racial bias, researcher Carla R. Monroe points out,

Many teachers may not explicitly connect their disciplinary reactions to negative perceptions of Black males, yet systematic trends in disproportionality suggest that teachers may be implicitly guided by stereotypical perceptions that African American boys require greater control than their peers and are unlikely to respond to nonpunitive measures. (Quoted in Staats, 2015–2016, p. 31)

In another study of mindfulness training for educators, among a wide range of outcomes, teachers reported a tendency to evaluate challenging students in a more positive affective light (Taylor et al., 2015).

Positive Programs for Teachers

Several mindfulness programs have been developed specifically for teachers to combat teacher stress. The CARE (Cultivating Awareness and Resilience in Education) program was developed by education professor

Patricia Jennings, clinical child psychologist Christa Turksma, and contemplative education professor Richard C. Brown with support from the nonprofit Garrison Institute. It is a professional development program presented in five day-long sessions (the first four days are presented over four or five weeks, and the fifth session is given several months later). Teachers learn about the neuroscience of emotion, engage in small-group and self-reflection activities, and practice mindful strategies for boosting their social and emotional effectiveness as educators. After learning how to use the breath to focus attention, they learn to direct that attention toward other activities, such as standing in front of the classroom and walking and listening to others. Mindful listening practices can help teachers learn how to listen to others without feeling the urge to interrupt, without wanting to offer advice, and without judging the speaker. Facilitators coach teachers by phone and e-mail between sessions to help them practice and apply their new skills.

An evaluation of this program using a randomized controlled study design revealed significant improvement in teacher well-being, efficacy, stress with relation to time and burnout, and mindfulness compared with the control group (Jennings, Frank, Snowberg, Coccia, & Greenberg, 2013). Another study of CARE using a cluster randomized control design involving 36 elementary schools and 224 teachers demonstrated positive effects on adaptive emotional regulation, mindfulness, psychological distress, time-related stress, and emotional support in the classroom. This latter factor was especially evident in urban schools with at-risk populations (Jennings et al., 2017). A teacher who had participated in the CARE program observed:

> The thing that has changed me the most has been just learning about the whole emotional process and how everything works because now when my kids get upset I don't get upset. I'm just like, "Okay, well, go take a break and come back when you're calm," and before that's not what would happen. [Before] they would elevate me to the same level . . . it could happen in a matter of seconds, where I would be fine one second and you're doing something and now I'm totally angry and can't make a good decision about how I'm going to react, but now that's not the case anymore. . . . (Sharp & Jennings, 2015, p. 214)

A second program for K–12 teachers and administrators that has pioneered the training of teachers in mindfulness is Stress Management and Relaxation Techniques (SMART) in Education, which was developed with support from the Impact Foundation. It is based upon the Mindfulness-Based Stress Reduction program of the Center for Mindfulness at the University of Massachusetts Medical School and focuses on three main themes: (1) concentration, attention, and mindfulness; (2) awareness and understanding of emotions; and (3) empathy and compassion. Training consists of eight sessions spread over 11 weeks, including two day-long sessions. Participants are assigned 10 to 30 minutes of daily mindfulness practice. The results of this program have also been positive. Two randomized wait-list studies (in which the control group was on a waiting list to receive the program after the conclusion of the study) reported decreased occupational stress, anxiety, depression, and burnout and increased working-memory capacity, greater mindfulness and levels of self-compassion, and more focused attention (Roeser et al., 2013).

Other studies using comparable training methods have found similar positive results. In one study conducted at the Center for Healthy Minds at the University of Wisconsin, for example, teacher participants showed elevated levels of self-compassion and a decrease in psychological ills such as anxiety, depression, and burnout and also demonstrated greater teacher effectiveness in behavior management skills and in emotional and instructional support for students (Flook, Goldberg, Pinger, Bonus, & Davidson, 2013). Commenting on this study, Zakrzewski (2013) observed, "The study suggests that when teachers practice mindfulness, students' misbehavior and other stressors become like water off a duck's back, allowing them to stay focused on what teachers really want to do: teach." (For a comprehensive synthesis of several current studies on mindfulness for educators, see Emerson et al., 2017.)

How to Get Started with Your Own Practice

Some teachers may balk at the idea of starting a mindfulness practice, not sure when they're going to find the time to practice or how they're going to mobilize the discipline necessary to stay at it on a daily basis over the long term. The best way to get started is to start now and start small. Even a three-to-five-minute session can show significant results over time. James Butler, Austin (Texas) Independent School District Teacher of the Year, squeezes five minutes of time into his schedule while he's waiting for his coffee to steep:

> I have that five minutes and I can just sit down and breathe while the coffee is getting ready. . . . It doesn't have to be a one-day silent retreat. Just having a simple tiny teeny practice, every day, that's awesome just so you know what it's like. So when you share with your kids, you can empathize, and that makes all the difference in the world. (Sung, 2018)

Another way to quickly make mindfulness practice a regular part of your routine is to choose an activity for the day and plan to be mindful while doing it. This could involve eating lunch, drinking coffee, walking to your classroom, or any other activity that you do every day (see Figure 4.2). For teachers who can't find five minutes during a busy school day, there are ways to "steal" a few moments here and there to experience some of the benefits of mindfulness, including feeling the warmth of the sun on your face, taking a sip of water and concentrating just on that, or walking from your car to the school and focusing only on the feeling of the soles of your feet as they step on the pavement.

A wide range of resources can help you get into the practice of mindfulness. *The New York Times* has a section on its website called "How to Meditate" that contains basic instructions and also several audio-guided practice clips (1-Minute Meditation, 4-Minute Meditation, 10-Minute Meditation, and 15-Minute Meditation). It can be found at https://www.nytimes.com/guides/well/how-to-meditate?module=inline. In addition, a range of smartphone apps will lead you through a session of mindfulness, including Headspace (www.headspace.com) and Calm (www.calm.com). High school teacher Mary Davenport (2018) reports on her experience:

> First and foremost, I focus every day on my own practice of mindfulness through regular use of an app, attendance at retreats, and reading research. As teachers, we know our students can spot a fake within three seconds flat. If the mindfulness practice in the classroom feels fake, meaningful engagement decreases.

Figure 4.2

Five-Minute Mindful Coffee Break for Teachers

— Get a cup of coffee (or tea, hot chocolate, or some other hot drink) and then find a place in the school where you won't be disturbed.

— Before you take your first sip, close your eyes and feel the warmth of the cup (or mug) in your hands. Breathe in the aroma of the beverage. Feel the steam on your face. Notice your feelings of anticipation about taking a drink.

— Open your eyes and take your first sip. Be aware of the heat of the liquid on your lips and tongue. Notice the taste. Swish the liquid around in your mouth and feel the sensations it makes.

— Swallow the liquid, tracing the warmth all the way down your throat, esophagus, and stomach. Can you feel the warmth in your stomach?

— Take more sips, paying close attention to the sensations of taste, smell, and touch as you enjoy your coffee break.

Appendix B contains a list of books, CDs, apps, and organizations you can access for information on getting started with a mindfulness practice. Your community likely has resources including mindfulness groups, retreats, and programs that can support you as you're getting started. Some people find it helpful to begin a practice with a partner, such as a colleague at school, so that you can support each other. Several schoolwide mindfulness programs have begun through the efforts of one or two motivated teachers who have shared their excitement with other teachers and administrators (see Chapter 8).

Make sure that you go into a mindfulness practice with realistic expectations. Understand that it won't necessarily make you feel instantly relaxed or propel you into a state of oneness with all humanity. In fact, prepare yourself for lots of mind chatter and having to repeatedly focus your attention back on your breathing (or walking, eating, or other object of focus). Over time, you'll find that you become calmer, less reactive, and more focused and acquire habits of mind that make your instructional day easier and more fulfilling. As one student teacher put it after taking an introductory course on mindfulness,

At first, I struggled with the silence and centering because I am one of those people who likes to always be doing something. . . . However, after a few weeks of doing it, I learned to really appreciate the fact that there was some time during my day where it was perfectly acceptable for me to just relax and not have to be doing anything. (Quoted in Dorman, 2015, pp. 110–111)

Teachers have never had so many responsibilities in school. As Patricia Jennings puts it, "[Teachers] need a level of social-emotional competence that's way above the norm. . . . The average person, you couldn't stick them in a classroom with 25 kids and expect them to be successful as a teacher" (Will, 2017). Mindfulness represents a powerful tool that can help teachers meet the challenges of 21st century education. Alison Smith, a 4th grade teacher who now offers life coaching to teachers, notes that "as great as it is to get training on pedagogy, none of it really matters if you can't cope with the realities of the classroom" (Will, 2017). Some teachers may think that focusing so much attention on their own self-care diverts attention away from care of the students, but Baltimore kindergarten teacher Danna Thomas observes, "Self-care is not selfish. That's something I have to remind teachers because so often we put ourselves last" (Will, 2017).

Remember to put on your own oxygen mask *first*, and then you'll have the capacity to help your students put on theirs.

Takeaways

• Teachers are under unprecedented levels of stress due to disruptive and stressed students, accountability for standardized test results, school violence, and other demands on their time and energy.

• Stressed teachers devote less time to teacher-facilitated academic instruction to the whole class, spend less time planning and organizing their instruction, and experience greater conflict in teacher-child relationships. They also tend to have students with poorer academic outcomes.

• Creating a personal mindfulness practice can help teachers relate to students in a calm and centered way, reduce implicit biases toward at-risk students, and function more effectively with administrators, parents, and colleagues under conditions of high stress.

- Programs that train educators in personal mindfulness, such as CARE (Cultivating Awareness and Resilience in Education) and SMART (Stress Management and Relaxation Techniques) in Education, have outcomes that include decreased occupational stress, anxiety, depression, and burnout; increased working-memory capacity, greater mindfulness, and higher levels of self-compassion and well-being; and more focused attention.

- The best way to begin a mindfulness practice is to start small and start now. A range of resources is available for educators, including online guided mindfulness sessions and mindfulness phone apps, retreats, and classes. Even sessions as simple as a five-minute mindful coffee break can result in positive outcomes. One good way to begin is to practice with a colleague or a support group.

5

Teaching Kindness and Compassion

A Native American parable has a grandfather explaining to his grandson: "There are two wolves at war inside everyone. One is greedy, mean, and angry. The other is generous, kind, and friendly." The grandson asks, "Which one will win?" The grandfather answers, "The one you feed."

Parents and teachers tell kids to be kind to one another, but they usually don't show them how. Mindfulness brings with it a growing awareness of the broad range of feelings that arise within us concerning other people and ourselves. The practice of loving kindness and compassion complements mindfulness—as we become aware of how we project negative feelings onto others (or ourselves), we feel an innate desire to change the pattern and to generate warm feelings of kindness.

Society's Kindness Crisis

We certainly need kindness in our frenetic, achievement-oriented society. According to a study from the Harvard Graduate School of Education, nearly 80 percent of students rank achievement or happiness over caring for others (Berkowicz & Myers, 2014). In a survey commissioned by the children's magazine *Highlights*, 44 percent of respondents said their parents most wanted them to be happy, 33 percent said their parents' top priority was for them to do well in school, and only 23 percent said their parents most wanted them to be kind (Blad, 2017). These figures contrast sharply with those related to parents' own wishes for their kids. In a national survey of 2,502 parents conducted by the Center for Healthy Minds at the University of Wisconsin–Madison with the cooperation of writers, producers, and educators from the TV program *Sesame Street*, nearly 80 percent agreed with the statement that "it's more important that my children are kind to others" than "academically successful" (Spoon, 2017). Developmental psychologist Luba Falk Feigenberg commented on the *Highlights* survey, saying, "Kids are hearing that parents want them to be focused on achievement. . . . It's tough because there are so many messages about individual success and achievement in particular that overpower the messages parents think they are actually sending about being caring and kind" (Blad, 2017).

One consequence of failing to prioritize the practice of kindness in our culture is the chronic problem of bullying in schools. According to government statistics, over 70 percent of young people say they have witnessed bullying in their school, and 62 percent of school staff have witnessed bullying at least twice in the previous two months. Perhaps most significant, only 20 to 30 percent of students who are bullied report to an adult that they have been bullied (Stopbullying.gov, 2017). Among social media users, 88 percent of teens have seen someone be mean or cruel on a social network (Lenhart, Madden, Smith, Purcell, & Zickuhr, 2011). Although anti-bullying programs may help ameliorate this situation to some degree, they may not get at the heart of the problem. According to Williams College professors Susan Engel and Marlene Sandstrom,

> [T]he danger of anti-bullying laws, which have now been passed by all but six states, is that they may subtly encourage schools to address this complicated problem quickly and superficially. Many schools are buying expensive anti-bullying curriculum packages, big glossy binders that look reassuring on the bookshelf and technically place schools closer to compliance with the new laws. But our research on child development makes it clear that there is only one way to truly combat bullying. As an essential part of the school curriculum, *we*

have to teach children how to be good to one another, how to cooperate, how to defend someone who is being picked on and how to stand up for what is right. (Engel & Sandstrom, 2010, italics added)

The Benefits of Being Mindfully Compassionate

Developing the ability to be kind to others is an important skill for social and emotional competence. In one study, students ages 9 to 11 were asked to perform three acts of kindness while a control group did an activity that involved mapping places they had visited. The students in the kindness group experienced improved well-being and greater peer popularity (as measured by sociometric peer ratings) compared to the control group (Layous, Nelson, Oberle, Schonert-Reichl, & Lyubomirsky, 2012). A prospective study of 753 kindergartners (half of them in a high-risk group) found that teachers' ratings of students' prosocial skills predicted outcomes in young adulthood (13 to 19 years later) related to education, employment, criminal activity, substance use, and mental health (Jones, Greenberg, & Crowley, 2015). As one team of positive psychology researchers put it, "Acts of kindness can build trust and acceptance between people, encourage social bonds, provide givers and receivers with the benefits of positive social interaction, and enable helpers to use and develop personal skills and thus themselves" (Kerr, O'Donovan, & Pepping, 2015, p. 20).

As noted previously, the effect of having enhanced awareness through mindfulness practice is complementary to the experience of compassion. As students develop their ability to focus, they also build their capacity to sustain universal, nonreferential love and compassion. At the same time, feeling kindness and love for others helps an individual develop a peace of mind that is useful for entering into a focused state. The practice of mindfulness can lead to feelings of self-compassion (viewing emotions without judgment), which can radiate to love for and less judgment of others. Ultimately, mindfulness involves the development of empathy and compassion while being fully present in the moment.

A big part of this kindness campaign involves self-compassion. Educators Laura Pinger and Lisa Flook (2016) note,

We can . . . help kids reflect on their emotions, which sometimes feel overwhelming, and change their relationship to them. After a child calms down, we can sit with them and reflect on that feeling. Which part of the body felt angry, happy, or upset? All emotions are natural, so kids shouldn't feel bad about experiencing them; we can teach them to cultivate a kinder attitude.

Self-compassion skills are especially crucial for adolescents, who experience acute levels of critical self-consciousness ("I looked stupid in math class today," "They looked at me like I'm a loser") that can become highly toxic and lead to mental health problems (Armstrong, 2016). In one meta-analysis of studies related to self-compassion and psychological distress in adolescents, a large effect size was found pointing to an inverse relationship between self-compassion and anxiety, depression, and stress (Marsh, Chan, & MacBeth, 2018).

In one randomized controlled study, students ages 14 to 17 who took a program entitled "Making Friends with Yourself: A Mindful Self-Compassion Program for Teens" demonstrated greater outcomes related to self-compassion and life satisfaction and significantly lower instances of depression than the control group, with trends toward greater mindfulness, greater social connectedness, and lower anxiety (Bluth et al., 2016). The program uses mindfulness techniques, guided imagery visualizations, meditations, taking photos of positive images, writing a self-affirming pledge of core values, and other strategies for cultivating self-compassion in teens. Another study concluded, interestingly, that self-compassion moderates against the negative effects of low self-esteem by accepting self-doubt, negative self-evaluations, and adversity as part of the human condition (Marshall et al., 2015). Research also suggests that self-compassion is associated with lower levels of stress-induced inflammation as measured by concentrations of a substance called interleukin-6 in blood plasma (Breines et al., 2014).

A Curriculum of Kindness

Educators have been busy creating programs that teach kindness and compassion. Laura Pinger and Lisa Flook and their colleagues at the

Center for Healthy Minds at the University of Wisconsin–Madison (2017) have developed a "kindness curriculum" for preschool students that has been disseminated widely (a free copy is available at https:// centerhealthyminds.org/join-the-movement/sign-up-to-receive-the -kindness-curriculum) and even adopted by *Sesame Street* as part of its yearlong theme, "K is for Kindness." The curriculum is a 12-week program (two sessions per week) in which students learn the skills of mindfulness practice and keep track of their acts of kindness on a "Kindness Garden" poster in the classroom. Flook and Pinger (n.d.) write: "The idea is that friendship is like a seed—it needs to be nurtured and taken care of in order to grow. Through that exercise, we got students talking about how kindness feels good and how we might grow more friendship in the classroom." Kids learn to communicate compassionately with each other by having one person hold a "peace wand" decorated with a heart and "speak from the heart" while the other student holds a wand with a star and listens to what the first child has said and then repeats it back to her.

The curriculum also contains books on the theme of kindness, kindness songs, movement activities, and discussions about kindness. For example, after reading the book *Sumi's First Day of School Ever,* the story of an immigrant student who struggles with English, the children brainstorm ways they could help Sumi adjust to her new environment with an action as simple as a smile. "At the heart of the discussion is empowering young children to begin to feel how positive qualities such as kindness and gratitude feel in their bodies, physically," says Flook. "This is where a mindful approach comes in—the skills build on paying attention to the body and extend to offering kind attention to ourselves and the world around us" (quoted in Spoon, 2017). A randomized controlled study of the effectiveness of this preschool "kindness curriculum" determined that the intervention group showed greater improvements in social competence and earned higher report card grades in domains of learning, health, and social-emotional development, whereas the control group exhibited more selfish behavior over time (Flook, Goldberg, Pinger, & Davidson, 2015).

Projects That Encourage Kindness

A wide range of other programs in the United States and elsewhere seek to develop the themes of kindness, empathy, and tolerance in their students. Education expert Molly Barker teaches these skills at the primary school level by taking pairs of cast-off shoes and labeling them "poor," "rich," "boy," "girl," "homeless," "physically disabled," "old," "young," "sick," "from a different country," "different religion," "different ethnicity," and "different political beliefs." She then asks the kids to literally "walk in another person's shoes" (Miller, 2012) and then discuss their feelings and thoughts. Sixth grade students at Reed Intermediate School in Newtown, Connecticut, work individually or in small groups to create "kindness carts." Each cart is an enterprise for making money (e.g., a taco stand, a lemonade stand, a dog treats cart), and the proceeds fund a worthy cause. In one instance the funds went toward building a well in Zubah Town, Liberia (Hallabeck, 2018).

Students at Frank Wagner Elementary School in Monroe, Washington, observe Kindness Week around Valentine's Day; staff and students write kind notes to each other, thank local agencies for keeping the community safe, and gather at a schoolwide assembly to recognize students who went above and beyond in kindness (Sullivan, 2018). A Canada-based program, the Roots of Empathy, brings a mother and baby along with a facilitator into the classroom once a month to help students understand the importance of caring for others and responding positively to changing emotional states (Schachter, 2011). Schools involved in the Great Kindness Challenge reserve one week a year to engage in a range of kindness-related activities, including holding kindness assemblies, hosting a kindness-themed essay contest, organizing a flash-mob dance to a kindness-related song during recess or an open period, and passing out "caught you being kind" cards to students demonstrating kindness behaviors (to learn more, go to https://thegreatkindnesschallenge.com/schooledition/).

Schools involved in the Middle School Kindness Challenge, a project of the nonprofit group Stand for Children, take part in kindness-related lessons and create their own kindness rituals, such as establishing a kindness club or sponsoring a kindness expo (Dalbey,

2018). At Riverside Intermediate School in Fishers, Indiana, students were offered another type of challenge: to complete 500 compassionate acts in one month. To keep track of how many acts of kindness they'd accomplished, the teacher posted a giant thermometer (like those used to chart contributions in a fund drive) and students added color with each individual or collective act of kindness. Compassionate acts included writing notes of encouragement and then leaving them in library books, on desks, in lockers, and in other areas where students would find them (Bream, 2018). At Worcester (Massachusetts) Technical High School, students created buddy benches for elementary schools; the benches are for students to sit on when they feel lonely and want a friend to play with, though they also use the benches to read or to visit with friends (Monfredo, 2018).

Tips for Integrating Kindness into the Classroom

In addition to the ideas and programs shared in this chapter, educators can use a number of other strategies to integrate kindness and compassion into the school day. Here are some suggestions.

• *Model compassion in your own teaching.* If you tell your students to be kind but then yell at them when they misbehave, you're not being a very good role model (unless you also model self-compassion by forgiving yourself for losing your temper). Kyle Redford, a 5th grade teacher at Marin Country Day School in Corte Madera, California, writes:

> This year, I decided to go toward the most difficult students with additional compassion, rather than retreating in frustration when my initial attempts to change them failed. . . . [My] new plan asked questions that were less canned, free of scolding or shame, and more gentle and genuine. Are you feeling all right? Is something bothering you? What was last night like? Did you get enough sleep? Do you want to talk? (Redford, 2018)

Having your own mindfulness practice can go a long way toward helping you develop the centeredness necessary to approach students with a kind attitude.

• *Consider bringing a pet into the classroom.* Pets elicit a natural sense of compassion from children. The long-term caring for a pet offers the opportunity to learn what to do when one's kindness is being challenged. It also offers opportunities for sharing responsibilities with peers and experiencing a sense of caring beyond one's own self. Pets in the Classroom is an educational grant program that guides teachers in securing funding for bringing a small animal into their classroom (to learn more, go to https://www.petsintheclassroom .org/).

• *Engage students in community service projects.* Service learning has been a part of the educational landscape for decades, but its role in eliciting feelings of kindness and compassion in students is less well known. Helping students identify problems that need tending to in their community or in the wider world can awaken a desire to help others in need. Projects to consider include community beautification, canned-food drives for a local pantry, fundraising for communities in underdeveloped nations, helping out after natural disasters, building homes for low-income families, assisting with voter registration, or volunteering to visit the elderly.

• *Have regular class discussions.* Plan time on a daily or weekly basis when students can air their feelings about a broad range of social issues and can practice communication skills that embody kindness, compassion, and respect for one another. Lourdes Ramirez, who teaches 6th grade social studies in Hudson, Massachusetts, uses morning meetings to address bullying and other social issues, asking questions such as "How would you respond if a friend shared that she's being picked on? What are the words you can say?" and "What is your responsibility if someone comes to you with gossip?" (Schachter, 2011). Rachel Simmons, author and cofounder of Girls Leadership, volunteers teaching self-compassion at a local elementary school in Northampton, Massachusetts, where kindergartners, for example, share embarrassing moments ("I fell off the monkey bars in front of my friends") and then practice hugging themselves as a form of self-soothing (Simmons, 2018).

• *Practice affirmations and visualizations of kindness toward others.* In the Kindness Curriculum developed by the Center for

Healthy Minds at the University of Wisconsin-Madison, the 4-year-olds practice saying simple phrases such as "May I be safe, may I be happy, may I be healthy, may I be peaceful" for themselves and "May you be safe, may you be happy, may you be healthy, may you be peaceful" for their classmates. The curriculum's cocreators, Lisa Flook and Laura Pinger, go on to say that "these wishes can be extended further: to my entire classroom, my school, my neighborhood, my whole community. . . . May we all be safe, may we all be happy, may we all be healthy, may we all be peaceful" (Pinger & Flook, 2016). Jim Librandi, a 5th grade teacher at Greenwich School in Greenwich, Connecticut, encourages students to think a kind thought about a person they love and then to think a kind thought about someone who has upset them. "They . . . keep the thought private," Librandi said (*Greenwich Free Press*, 2017).

In one sense, kindness is a skill to be learned, like spelling or geography. "We can't assume that kids know how to be empathic," explains Amy Hamilton, a 3rd grade teacher at Mulready Elementary School in Hudson, Massachusetts. "We have to teach it" (Schachter, 2011). However, in another sense, kindness is something entirely different from a set of learned behaviors. The etymology of the word *kindness* shows that it's related to the words *kin* and *kindred*, suggesting that kindness defines a natural relationship among members of the same family, group, or species. In that sense, kindness is more of an instinct, perhaps one that was selected for in human evolution, where people who were kind to members of their own kin group contributed to the coherence and strength of their group and thus ensured their survival and the passing along of their genes for future generations (Wilson, 2000). As one little boy involved with the Center for Healthy Minds' Kindness Curriculum told his teacher, "Miss Lisa, I was born to be kind" (Canty, 2017). Kindness and compassion can't be grafted onto students or drilled into them like the multiplication tables; kindness and compassion need to be gently elicited. Children need to be *reminded* that they are intrinsically kind. Once that occurs, it seems that what takes place is a ripple effect across the child's social network, a cascade that can encompass a wider circle of compassionate individuals in the classroom, the school, the community, and, eventually perhaps, the entire world.

Takeaways

• Mindfulness and kindness are linked to each other in the sense that being less judgmental of our own experiences can make us less likely to judge others and instead be kind to them, and being kind to others can lead to greater serenity in our own mindfulness practices.

• There is a kindness crisis in our achievement-oriented culture, in which students rank academic achievement over caring for others. One result of this prioritization of values is bullying in the schools and on social networks.

• Kindness and compassion are associated with positive outcomes such as greater feelings of well-being and higher levels of peer popularity.

• Schools from preschool to high school have been involved in a wide range of programs and activities for promoting kindness and compassion in the classroom, including a Kindness Garden project, Kindness Week, buddy benches, kindness carts, an infant-in-the-classroom program, and a challenge to commit 500 acts of kindness in one week.

• Tips for engaging students in kind behaviors include modeling compassion as a teacher, bringing a pet into the classroom, engaging in service learning, and using affirmations (e.g., "May you be healthy, may you be happy, may you be peaceful").

• In one sense, kindness is a skill to be learned, like spelling or arithmetic; but in another sense, kindness is an innate instinct—one that perhaps allowed humans to evolve as social creatures—and one that needs to be elicited or drawn out through gentle encouragement.

6

Adapting to Students' Developmental Levels

Although mindfulness practices were originally developed for adults, most of the instructions are valid for younger participants. In this chapter, you'll learn how to adapt some aspects of the experience to fit the developmental needs of your students. One key adaptation is time. Expecting kindergartners to sit quietly and practice mindfulness for 20 minutes is absurd, so scale the time allotted to fit your students. Lafayette Elementary School in Washington, D.C., for example, incorporates up to 15 minutes of meditation every morning for 4th graders, but for 4- and 5-year-olds, "we usually stay calm for about one minute," according to Linda Ryden, the school's mindfulness instructor (Plantier, 2017). Another key adaptation is related to teaching related content. Though the mindfulness program MindUP includes information about the reticular activating system of the brain in its preK–2 curriculum (Scholastic, n.d.), I believe that the teaching of didactic material (e.g., the neuroscience of mindfulness and its underlying mechanisms) is more appropriately taken up in the later elementary grades, middle school, and high school.

These two modifications—time allotted and material taught—are the most general in a comprehensive collection of adaptations that need to be made as mindfulness is practiced at different grade levels. This chapter will explore some of these modifications and the developmental considerations that underlie them. It's worth remembering that many of the activities and adaptations considered here may be suitable for more than one developmental level (e.g., the "mind jar" described on p. 71 is appropriate for all grade levels).

Mindfulness in Early Childhood Education

In a sense, it's easier to teach mindfulness to young children because they are less involved in internal mind chatter and more connected to each present moment. It may be that this stage of development is the perfect window for teaching mindfulness practices. Just as research points to this age as ideal for teaching a new language or a musical instrument, a growing consensus concurs that this age is optimal for teaching social and emotional skills. The famous marshmallow experiment, in which children were promised two marshmallows later if they could resist eating one marshmallow during the experimenter's absence, helped pave the way to an understanding that self-regulatory ability at age 4 (indexed by waiting a longer time for a reward) predicted attentional capacity, self-control, and frustration tolerance during adolescence and adulthood (Eigsti et al., 2006; Mischel, 2015). Furthermore, economists have determined that investments in early childhood education more than pay for themselves over time, saving later costs in welfare, crime, mental health, and other social expenditures and resulting in as much as a 7 to 10 percent return per child, per year, for every dollar spent (Heckman, 2008; Heckman, 2011; Heckman, Moon, Pinto, Savelyev, & Yavitz, 2010).

Several recent randomized controlled studies have demonstrated that preschoolers and kindergartners can benefit from mindfulness programs. In the last chapter we discussed how preschoolers who had gone through the Kindness Curriculum program at the University of Wisconsin showed greater improvements in social competence and earned higher report card grades compared with the students in the control group (Flook et al., 2015). Similarly, preschoolers and kindergartners who have completed another mindfulness program showed improvements in teacher-reported executive-function skills specifically related to working memory, planning, and organizing, whereas students in a business-as-usual control group showed a decline in these areas. By the end of kindergarten, the mindfulness group also had higher vocabulary and reading scores compared with the control group (Lemberger-Truelove, Carbonneau, Atencio, Zieher, & Palacios, 2018).

But perhaps the best proof of the effect of mindfulness on young children comes from watching kids in context. Liz Slade, a kindergarten teacher at Chatsworth Elementary School in Larchmont, New York, observed a student who had practiced mindfulness walk up to a tall structure that her classmates had painstakingly created from building blocks. "I watched this little girl raise her foot to kick the blocks, take a breath and then walk away," she said. "The kids can learn to notice distraction, self-regulate, and ask themselves, 'What do I need?'" (Gerszberg, 2018).

The emphasis in mindfulness activities at the preK, kindergarten, and even lower-elementary levels should be on sensory-motor and gross-motor activities that are dynamic, engaging, and fun. Saltzman and Goldin (2008) recommend the following movement activity for when the kids start to get wiggly:

> Each child is a strand of seaweed anchored to the floor. Initially we are in a strong current, making big rapid movements. Gradually the current decreases, and our movements become smaller and smaller until there is very gentle swaying and then stillness. Throughout the Seaweed Practice, the children are gently reminded to be aware of their physical sensations, thoughts, and feelings. This practice simultaneously honors the children's natural need for movement and continues to develop their capacity to pay attention; in this exercise the focus of attention is on the experience of moving. (p. 149)

Early childhood is a good time also to introduce simple mindful stretching postures. At Westminster Center School in Westminster, Vermont, kindergarten teacher Vicky Peters turns mindful poses into play. "I'll be in down dog [a pose in which only the hands and feet are on the ground, making a bridge] and they'll go under" (Thomas, 2008, p. 20). Or she'll give the kids the opportunity to invent their own poses, which promotes creativity, individuality, and acceptance of differences. Finally, she also provides an alternative for kids who have trouble with nap time, giving them the option of doing quiet, gentle stretching poses in a special area of the room while the other kids nap.

The kids in Liz Slade's kindergarten class made up their own imagination breaths. Going around the circle, each child paired a unique hand movement with a breath and gave it an imaginative name such as "snowflake breath," "jellyfish breath," or "clamshell breath," which the other kids would mimic. When the kids got antsy, Slade asked them to get up and jump around. After working some of their wiggles out, she then asked them to "make a mindful statue"; the children froze in place and only the sound of their breathing could be heard (Gerszberg, 2018).

Another way of teaching mindfulness activity in a developmentally appropriate way in early childhood is to have the kids experience sensory activities while staying in touch with the present-moment quality of these experiences. Activities might include

• Feeling sand or pebbles pass through their fingers.
• Sticking their hands into "mystery boxes" that hold unseen objects with different textures.
• Listening to different "mystery sounds" of items like dried beans shaken in small covered containers.
• Inhaling scents from different ingredients (e.g., cinnamon and mint).
• Taking a walk and experiencing the smells, colors, and sounds in nature.
• Engaging in tactile experiences with finger paint or clay.

Virtually all the sensory-motor experiences that are part of any good early childhood program can be turned into mindfulness exercises simply by asking students to pay attention to the sensations they experience while they play or interact with different materials.

The explanations to young children about mindfulness should connect to imaginative themes. For example, a *Sesame Street* video shows the Count teaching a breathing technique to Cookie Monster by holding up five fingers, pretending they are birthday candles, and blowing them out in succession (Sesame Street in Communities, n.d.). Saltzman and Goldin (2008) explain mindfulness by telling a story about "a still quiet place" that exists inside each of us; we can go to this place whenever we want, safely talk about feelings (e.g., anger, sadness, and fear), and may find that these emotions aren't as big or powerful as they seemed.

Children's literature is also an excellent way to imaginatively teach basic principles of mind wandering and peacefulness. At Highland Presbyterian Church Nursery and Weekday School in Louisville, Kentucky, for example, kindergarten teacher Laura Patterson reads the book *Mindful Monkey, Happy Panda* by Lauren Alderfer to teach about mindfulness (Carter, 2015). The monkey, whose mind jumps all over the place, meets a panda who explains to him that real happiness results from focusing all one's attention on the now. (See Appendix B for a list of children's books related to mindfulness.)

Using props can impart ideas about mindfulness in simple and easily understood ways. The Kindness Curriculum developed by the University of Wisconsin's Center for Healthy Minds teaches preschoolers to pay attention to their breathing by balancing a stuffed toy, flat stone, bean bag, or small weighted object on their bellies when they lie down. Preschoolers are asked to rock their "belly buddies" to sleep with each inhalation and exhalation as they listen to relaxing music (Center for Healthy Minds, 2017). To teach the students about how busy a mind can get and how practice can help us calm it, the Kindness Curriculum uses a "mind jar," which is jar of water, a little glitter, and a drop of dish soap. When the jar is shaken, the glitter swirls. When the jar is at rest, the glitter settles—just like our minds do during mindfulness practice. This example is good for all ages.

Implementing Mindfulness in Elementary School

I've argued (Armstrong, 2006, 2007) that one important developmentally appropriate goal for students in elementary school is to learn how the world works. Kids at this age are hungry for explanations, rules, procedures, and descriptions that will help them interact more successfully with the world. Therefore, teaching them about mindfulness, how it helps combat stress, and the best ways to practice it should be given special emphasis. Once they begin practicing mindfulness, they'll see it as an important tool in creating a sense of well-being. Maggie Welp, a Compassionate Schools Project K–5 teacher with the Jefferson County Public Schools in Louisville, Kentucky, reports,

> One of our second-grade classes is really great about telling their teacher when they notice her starting to get frustrated with some-body. They will just call her out and tell her she needs to put her hands on her anchors [one hand on the belly and the other on the chest] and say we all need to take a break. It catches you so off guard when you have a seven-year-old telling you that, but it also shows you how much power the program is holding with them because even if they don't fully understand those concepts, they're getting those building blocks to get deeper and deeper as they get older. (Wagner, 2018)

There are many fun ways to explain mindfulness to kids at the elementary school level. Puppy training is one apt metaphor for describing how the mind wanders off and needs to be continually brought back to the present moment. The puppy tends to wander away from his paper just like our minds, so the trainer must patiently pick up the puppy and put him back on the paper over and over (there's even a children's book that presents this idea in a slightly modified form: *Puppy Mind*, by Andrew Jordan Nance). Another animal metaphor involves a cat and a mouse: "Close your eyes and say to yourself: 'I wonder what my next thought is going to be?' Then focus very carefully, waiting for the next thought—like a cat watching a mouse hole. I wonder what thought is going to come out of the mouse hole?" (Playfield Institute, n.d.). Saltzman and Goldin (2008) use the metaphor of the "thought parade" to describe the flow of our thoughts during mindfulness practice:

> [Children] begin to watch their thoughts go by as if they are watching a parade. They may notice that some thoughts are loud and brightly dressed, other thoughts are shy and lurk in the background, and still others come back again and again. When children notice they are marching with the parade (i.e., lost in thought), they are encouraged to return to the sidewalk and simply watch the thoughts go by. This practice supports children in watching their thoughts without believing them or taking them personally. (p. 150)

The Australian mindfulness program Smiling Mind uses the weather as a metaphor. School librarian Marie Curtis (2016) writes:

> [Children] examine how they are feeling inside (in terms of the weather). We have all kinds of weather—lots of sunny children, some cloudy and rainy and the occasional snowstorm or hurricane. The exercise helps children to come to understand that moods change and pass like the weather, and the cloudy and rainy children perk up with the thought that the sun might come out later.

For digital natives, the use of a tech metaphor may work well. In one study of children's perspectives of mindfulness practice, students were asked about their favorite parts of the mindfulness journey. One student wrote: "pressing on my pause button because it made me calm" (Ager, Albrecht, & Cohen, 2015, p. 906).

To introduce the central role of the breath in mindfulness, students might be asked to imagine that they have a balloon in their stomach that they repeatedly inflate and deflate. For other students, blowing bubbles may be helpful. This activity serves two purposes: first, to call attention to the importance of the breath; and second, to show students how bubbles are like our thoughts—some bigger than others, some lasting longer than others. Students might also practice their breathing by blowing into pinwheels to make them spin, or using straws to make objects move on their desks.

To ground the experience of breathing in a hands-on activity, some teachers suggest that students trace a circle on the palm of their hand as they breathe in and then trace the circle in the opposite direction as they breathe out. To externalize the process of breathing and lead students in their own mindful breathing, some teachers use a Hoberman sphere or "breath ball," a geodesic dome-like structure that can be expanded and contracted in the front of the class as students breathe in and out (see Willard & Nance, 2018). Some kids will come up with their own images for the process of breathing, as did one 3rd grader at St. Agnes Catholic School in Louisville, Kentucky, who commented, "When I'm thinking about mindfulness, I think of waves. When I breathe, the waves are rolling into the shore, and then when I breathe out, the waves are going back" (Carter, 2015).

Mindful stretching should be an important component of any elementary school mindfulness program. Here is a favorite pose that students might do, as described by Dana Santas (2016), one of the country's leading yoga trainers:

> *Dog at the fire hydrant*—Have students make an A-frame shape by bending over, straightening their legs, placing their arms in front of them, and pushing up their tailbones (this position is known as the "downward-facing dog pose"). Suggest that they lift and hold up one leg for a count of 10. Finally, ask them to switch legs for another count of 10 (the count can be longer or shorter, depending upon skill and age). Naturally, there will be giggles, but once they subside, the kids will love doing the pose again and again.

Make sure that once students are in a pose, you suggest that they focus on their breathing and bodily sensations. In this way the activity becomes mindful.

Because open space may be at a premium in a desk-filled elementary school classroom, it's useful to incorporate mindful stretching activities that can be done sitting down at a desk or standing up and using the desk as a stabilizing object. For sitting poses, students can do shoulder shrugs, which involve elevating their shoulders on the inhale and lowering their shoulders on the exhale. For "chest openers," they can lace their fingers behind their back or simply hold the back of their chair and lean back gently, inhaling while they lean back and exhaling as they come back to a normal sitting position. For a desk-supported pose while standing, students can place one hand on their desk and then take a step with one foot, bending their knee a little, holding their free arm up in the air and breathing in and out to a count of 5 (or 10). Then they can do the same thing with the opposite leg. This is a modified warrior pose (Landau, 2018).

Mindful walking is best conducted outdoors or in the school's gym or multipurpose room. Have each student select a small area where they can walk unimpeded for about five or six steps (or more, if space permits). Instruct them to take three breaths before starting, and then breathe normally and walk slowly within that area, focusing all their attention on the act of walking. Which part of their foot makes contact with the ground first? Are their legs heavy or light? What does the ground beneath their feet feel like? Can they feel the pressure of their socks or shoes while walking? Author and educator Susan Kaiser Greenland points out that if children are "particularly hyper, the really slow walking can be difficult for them. . . . In that case, have them go at whatever their natural speed is. They might need to let go of some excess energy" (Agsar, 2018). To add some variety to the exercise, suggest that your students imagine walking on eggshells, in molasses or honey, against a strong headwind, or on hot pavement. After a few sessions of mindful walking, suggest that students, instead of racing down the hallway between classes with lots of things on their mind, slow their pace and focus on putting one foot in front of the other—and even counting the steps if this helps.

Finally, create a routine for doing mindfulness practices by having a bell or a set of chimes on hand to initiate each session. A common practice is for a teacher to say something like this to the students just before ringing the bell: "I'd like you all to listen closely to the sound of the bell, and when you can no longer hear it, raise your hand. That will let me know we can begin our mindfulness practice." Then the students can begin watching their breathing, engage in mindful eating (a small piece of candy such as a Hershey's Kiss is a favorite), do a body scan (at this age, have students gently tighten the muscles of each part of the body as it is mentioned), or engage in mindful walking or stretching. A handy concept for this age level is the metaphor of the "tool kit," incorporating the idea that students have a range of strategies for dealing with stress. A tool kit might consist of activities such as taking three deep breaths, breathing in their favorite color, doing five shoulder shrugs, focusing on the tension in their body and watching it melt away, and watching their thoughts march by on parade. The idea that elementary school kids can have a repertoire of self-care strategies to go along with their textbooks, notebooks, folders, and pen and pencil boxes suggests that social and emotional skills are just as important as (or even more important than) academic skills.

The Challenge of Mindfulness in Middle School

Adolescence is when social and emotional learning becomes paramount because this is a time of life when students are particularly vulnerable to stress. Stress-reduction techniques that include mindfulness practices can help teens cope with the ups and downs of daily living. Early adolescence, in particular, is a bit tricky to work with as far as certain mindfulness practices are concerned, because students' acute self-consciousness makes them wary of doing things that will look odd to their peers. As one teen noted, "At first, I kind of rejected the practice because it made me too vulnerable, with its awkward poses and asking me to close my eyes. I didn't want to look—weird" (Machado, 2014). Yet mindfulness training may be exactly what students need to help smooth the contours of their emotion-tinged thinking processes and their difficulties with emotional self-regulation. Research suggests that mindfulness helps teens by improving their executive functioning, reducing their stress levels, increasing their positive emotions, decreasing their negative emotions, and promoting their general well-being (Bluth & Blanton, 2014; Broderick & Jennings, 2012; Sanger & Dorjee, 2016; Schonert-Reichl & Lawlor, 2010).

Young teens have attained Piaget's stage of formal operational thinking and are thus capable of engaging in fairly sophisticated metacognitive behavior (Piaget & Inhelder, 2013). This can be a time, therefore, when students begin to engage in one-word labeling of their thoughts, emotions, sensations, and perceptions, putting them into categories such as "planning" "remembering," "reflecting," and "judging." Similarly, this is a time when mindfulness training can include a good deal of information about the brain, stress physiology, self-care, neuroplasticity, and other relevant subjects. The developers of one mindfulness program for adolescents, Learning to Breathe, note that the program "capitalizes on youth's growing metacognitive skills by explicitly teaching about mindfulness . . . by helping youth recognize stress triggers and when to reduce chronic stress to prevent buildup (conditional knowledge); and by teaching them the skills via in-class and at-home mindfulness practice (procedural knowledge)" (Broderick & Frank, 2014, p. 27).

Dan Siegel (2015), clinical professor of psychiatry at UCLA, uses a simple hand model to explain the brain to adolescents. If one makes a fist, the wrist and arm represent the reptilian brain (controlling heart rate, breathing, body temperature, and balance); the thumb folded inside the hand is the limbic, or "emotional," brain; and the fingers enclosing it signify the neomammalian brain or neocortex (with the fingernails representing the most recently evolved part of the brain, the prefrontal cortex). Using this model, educators have a tool to describe how mindfulness works by facilitating communication between the prefrontal cortex and the limbic areas of the brain. As a resource, JoAnn Deak and Terrence Deak (2013) have written a book for adolescents, *The Owner's Manual for Driving Your Adolescent Brain*, that can be used in conjunction with mindfulness training for teenagers.

Young adolescents prefer to spend time with their peers rather than with adults or children (Armstrong, 2016), and this hunger for peer affiliation should be considered when building buy-in into a mindfulness program for young teens. One study of mindfulness with middle schoolers in Finland suggested that subjects were more likely to continue their mindfulness practice at home after the conclusion of the school-based program if they knew that their peers were doing the same thing (Volanen et al., 2015). Letting the students lead mindfulness sessions is a good way to enlist peer acceptance; so is giving them opportunities to lead younger or older kids. Adriana Chavarin, principal of Paul Ecke Elementary School in Encinitas, California, observed students at an assembly getting restless. Then a few 6th graders spontaneously began to lead the group in mindful stretching and breathing exercises. "Every kid in the audience quieted down," says David Miyashiro, the district superintendent (Glazer, 2011). Similarly, Rosie Waugh, math teacher and mindfulness coordinator at McLean School in Potomac, Maryland, leads a mindfulness club and sometimes takes the 7th grade boys to the local elementary school to speak about mindfulness and to demonstrate "the mind jar" (Gerszberg, 2018).

Another potential challenge in implementing mindfulness in middle school and high school is the fragmentation of the school day into several different classes and teachers. If a school has a homeroom system, the homeroom teacher might be the best one to teach mindfulness skills. But mindfulness can also be quite effective as a transition tool when used to begin or end a class period to help students calm down and focus.

One middle school teacher ends each class with a three-to-five-minute exercise in which she asks students to close their eyes and focus on their breath. Then she asks them to think about what they've learned and accomplished that day, and ends by telling them how hard the class worked, how proud she is of them, and how she cares for them (Beach, n.d.). In another case, a middle school science teacher starts the school year by introducing a new mindfulness practice each week. Then, during the year, he lets the students pick which centering approach will work best for them (Sung, 2018). That's another important ingredient for buy-in—empowering students to call the shots and decide whether they want to participate. One teacher puts it this way: "Very importantly, I emphasize that students are never required to participate in any of the practices that I teach. In fact, I explicitly say, 'I am not the boss of what happens inside your head'" (Dorman, 2015, p. 108).

Mindfulness in High School

As noted throughout this book, kids of all ages are living with unprecedented levels of stress. But it seems as if high school students win the prize for being the most stressed. One high school senior was asked to list all his responsibilities on any given day and came up with this list: "Be on time. Homework. Applications. Scholarship essays. Two jobs: Chipotle and Macy's. Mentoring a younger student. Driving lessons. Exhausting" (Resnick, 2017). High school students have stresses from peer groups, dating partners, social networking, academic demands, and home strife, and in many cases also have to deal with bullying, poverty, crime, disabling health conditions, and crippling conditions such as depression, anxiety disorders, and eating disorders. In addition, the roller coaster that is called puberty is still wreaking havoc inside their changing bodies. Clearly, mindfulness represents a gift for helping to alleviate their troubles. As one high school junior put it:

High school is really stressful. . . . A lot of things can stack up on you, so it's nice to take a breath once in a while. And also in high school you kind of feel like a crappy person all the time because of just society, and like you wonder if you're cool or not, but none of that really matters. When we practice mindfulness, we're only worried about what we think about ourselves. (Sung, 2018)

One of the best ways to introduce mindfulness to high school students is by explaining how it will help them in their lives. As mindfulness teacher Patrick Cook-Deegan (2014) points out, "If you do not make mindfulness relevant to the lives of teenagers outside the class, they are not going to be engaged." Don't preach to them about its benefits, but rather let them begin practicing mindfulness so that they can prove to themselves that it really does work. Then serve as a facilitator as students share stories about its many benefits. High school English teacher Mary Davenport (2018) writes: "I hear phrases like these from students: 'Guess what? I practiced mindfulness before my soccer game' and 'Mindfulness helped me with my presentation' and 'I used mindfulness before I went to sleep last night.'" Bella Gleim, a 9th grader at McLean School, comments on her personal experience with mindfulness: "I thought it was weird at first [but then] I realized that it totally helped . . . with everything in my life." Instead of blanking out during a test, she can breathe for a minute. "Then I'm totally focused, the answers are coming back, and that way I can finish my test confidently" (Berl, 2015).

An effective way of making mindfulness practice look enticing to high school students (and younger kids) is by explaining how it is being used by professional sports teams, Hollywood movie stars, and other celebrities. The practitioners of mindfulness and other meditation techniques include a long list of luminaries: Oprah Winfrey, Liv Tyler, Jerry Seinfeld, Goldie Hawn (who has created her own mindfulness program for schools, called MindUP), Ellen DeGeneres, Paul McCartney, Lady Gaga, Nicole Kidman, Katy Perry, and Big Sean. Professional athletes who practice mindfulness include Kobe Bryant, Michael Jordan, Kendrick Lamar, and LeBron James. Dana Santos is a body-mind coach who works with several professional football, basketball, baseball, and hockey teams. As Stephen Curry, whom some consider the greatest basketball player of all time, told *The New York Times*, "You got to continue to just stay in the moment. When you stay in the moment, good things happen, because everybody's just wrapped up in the process" (quoted in Boyce, 2015).

Technology is another promising road into the world of the 21st century teenager. Mindfulness researcher Amy Saltzman has adolescents do a mindfulness exercise using their smartphones as the central object of contemplation. She asks them to "[f]eel the phone in your hand and notice your thoughts, feelings, urges, hopes, and fears." Then she lays out the next steps: "Press the home screen button and notice your thoughts, feelings, urges, hopes, and fears. Now simply open one social media app and look at only the first three posts. Notice your experience, your thoughts, and feelings. Turn your phone over and notice again your thoughts and feelings" (Ruiz, 2018). She then facilitates a discussion about their experiences, explaining how the internet is designed to be addicting by stimulating the release of the neurotransmitter dopamine, which encourages us to keep using it.

This same love affair with technology, however, can be turned to good use for mindfulness practice. As one teacher was guiding a high school class through their first experience with mindful breathing, several of the students were busy downloading a meditation app called Calm on their phones (Boccella, 2018). Although more than 10,000 self-care apps have been developed to help users become less depressed and anxious, fewer than 1 percent of these programs have been evaluated. In a survey of 560 apps specifically designed for mindfulness practice, only 23 were found to do more than simply remind the user to meditate, time their meditation, or offer support beyond a guided meditation track. Of those 23, Headspace was the study's top-scoring app; Smiling Mind, an Australian app, came in second (Ward, 2018). See Appendix B for a list of helpful mindfulness apps.

Another meditation exercise that employs students' smartphones requires them to take a walk with their phone or digital camera and snap 5 to 10 photos of things they find interesting and 1 photo of something that seems out of place. This helps them to better notice their surroundings. As psychotherapist Gina Biegel puts it, "They're going to be with the device anyway, so I might as well teach them to be mindful with it" (Agsar, 2018).

Takeaways

• Mindfulness was originally developed for adult use, so it's especially important for educators to think carefully about how to adapt or modify existing practices to suit the developmental needs of different age groups.

• Early childhood is a good time to introduce mindfulness activities that involve sensory-motor experiences such as mindful stretching, vivid displays of how the mind can become calmer with practice (e.g., shaking a jar filled with glitter and then watching the glitter settle), and props for self-monitoring breathing such as a belly buddy (a stone or a bean bag placed on the stomach that rises with each inhalation and lowers with each exhalation).

• Mindfulness at the elementary school level should be seen as part of a broader tool kit of social and emotional learning strategies that students can use for emotional self-regulation. Students can learn mindfulness principles using imaginative metaphors (e.g., emotions as weather, the thought parade) and hands-on activities for becoming conscious of the breath (e.g., blowing bubbles, making a pinwheel spin, moving light objects by blowing into a straw).

• As middle school students become increasingly capable of metacognition, it becomes more appropriate to teach them how the brain works and to instruct them in stress physiology and such mindfulness-related principles as thought labeling. Activities include peer-led mindfulness and the use of mindfulness practices during transitions between classes.

• High school students want to know how mindfulness is going to help them in their busy, stressful daily lives, so the emphasis should be on practice and sharing the results. Also, high schoolers are more likely to be enthused about mindfulness when they use technology-related mindfulness apps and when they learn about the use of mindfulness by professional athletes, movie stars, and other celebrities.

7

Applying in the Content Areas

One of the biggest concerns that teachers have about mindfulness is that it will take valuable time and energy away from curriculum content. By shifting the focus to something other than academics, many teachers believe that students will somehow fall behind in their studies and be at a disadvantage with respect to final grades and high-stakes testing. As far as some teachers are concerned, mindfulness is just another distraction that has come along as the fad of the moment to divert them from their true vocation, which is to teach. This concern needs to be taken seriously, because it can undermine efforts to make mindfulness a cornerstone of the learning process.

Mindfulness: A Key Learning Tool

The truth is that mindfulness supports academic learning in several ways (Lin & Mai, 2018; Mrazek et al., 2013). First, the brief time that is taken away from academics to practice mindfulness (sometimes as little as one or two minutes) pays off in terms of better focus once students return to their studies. So, for example, when kids transition from one class to another (or from one activity to another), their minds are often still on the earlier activity, especially if they're coming into the classroom from recess, lunch, or a more active class such as physical education. Similarly, at the start of a class session, many students are focused on future events: an upcoming test, what they'll do when school gets out, a personal issue with a classmate. It takes time for many kids to shift their focus back to the demands of the new class, and this distraction eats into valuable instructional time. Mindfulness helps students recenter themselves in preparation for their new tasks and activities.

A second way that mindfulness supports academics is by helping students overcome test anxiety. For some students, during testing "the mind becomes flooded with concerns about the possibility of failure," says Gerardo Ramirez, an assistant professor in developmental and cognitive psychology at the University of California, Los Angeles. "These worries essentially create a competition for attention between the worries and [the] need to solve the problems on the test" (Sparks, 2017). This stalemate results in a phenomenon that cognitive psychologists refer to as "choking," when the mind becomes totally overwhelmed and just shuts down. James Butler, an antistress consultant in Austin, Texas, shared an instance of this sort of reaction: "Last week, there was a 4th grader who just started crying and wouldn't write much on the test at all" (Sparks, 2017). Research has demonstrated that training in mindfulness practice helps students with test anxiety (see, for example, Bellinger, DeCaro, & Ralston, 2015; Cho, Ryu, Noh, & Lee, 2016; Shahidi, Akbari, & Zargar, 2017). Figure 7.1 describes a simple one-minute mindfulness routine that students can use before or during the taking of a test.

A third way that mindfulness contributes to better academic performance is by improving cognitive functions that are critical for successful learning, including working memory, planning, reflection, self-regulation, and attention. Clearly, if students aren't paying attention to their lessons, they won't do well academically. One study suggested that students' "attention failures" predicted their SAT scores (Unsworth, McMillan, Brewer, & Spillers, 2012). In a randomized controlled study of mindfulness with 5th and 6th graders, the mindfulness group scored higher than controls on measures of executive functions and also significantly outperformed controls with respect to their end-of-year math grades (Schonert-Reichl et al., 2015). Another study

Figure 7.1

One-Minute Mindful Test-Taking Routine for Students

— Before you start working on the test, close your eyes and focus your attention on the contact your feet make with the floor. Feel the pressure of your
body against the chair you're sitting in.

— Take three deep, slow breaths, focusing on the passage of air through your
nostrils or the rising and falling of your belly or chest with each inhalation
and exhalation.

— Open your eyes and focus on the test in front of you. Notice the color and
texture of the paper. Feel the shape of the pen or pencil that you're holding.
Say to yourself, "I'm going to do my very best on this test."

— Begin to take the test. If you become anxious or unsure of yourself at any
time during the test or you feel your mind wandering or getting confused
or impatient, repeat this exercise.

involving students in a fully automated mindfulness program (using
an audio recording) that took only 10 minutes per school day demonstrated improvements in quarterly grades in reading and science compared with a control group, without disrupting teaching operations
(Bakosh, Snow, Tobias, Houlihan, & Barbosa-Leiker, 2016).

Finally, mindfulness can improve academic performance when it
is directly integrated into course content. There are many practical
ways in which mindfulness might be interwoven with reading, math,
science, history, and other school subjects. The rest of the chapter
explores these possibilities.

The Joys of Mindful Reading

Just as there are practices of mindful breathing, walking, eating, and
stretching, there can be mindful reading. In this case, we make the
act of reading our central focus and become aware of when our minds
wander. Of course, a certain amount of mind wandering is a good thing
when it is directly related to the content of our reading (e.g., when we're
making connections between the text and our experiences). But often,
and especially in poor readers, the mind wanders to irrelevant matters
and loses contact with the text entirely. The ability to monitor when
this happens is an important component of mindful reading, as is simple awareness of the experience of reading. *New York Times* journalist

and mindfulness expert David Gelles (2017) suggests a scenario that we can follow from the moment we pick up a book:

> As you turn the pages, notice the quality of light, the color and even the smell of the ink on the page, the way that the spine of your book feels against the palms of your hands. You may find yourself more easily bored or sleepy. Take note: This is you slowing down—the point of this exercise to begin with. . . . Notice as reading causes your thoughts to meander. Reading does not have to be a comprehensive or linear exercise. Your mind is not a vacuum sweeping up each word mechanically. You will invariably drift off, think of something else, imagine what you're getting for lunch, or what you should have said to your date last night—all of this is expected. When your mind wanders, gently usher yourself back to the text and keep going.

There's actually a term in literacy studies that encompasses mindfulness: *deep reading*. The term was coined by literary critic Sven Birkerts. He defines deep reading as the slow and meditative possession of a book (Birkerts, 2006). This approach is in contrast to reading in the internet age, when speed, acquisition of information, and quick inspectional reading seem to be favored. Although deep reading involves many different skills, including the ability to reflect, interpret, empathize, analyze, and infer, one of its most important attributes is mindfulness. As Hall and her colleagues (2015) point out, "deep reading requires human beings to call upon and develop attentional skills, to be thoughtful and fully aware . . ." (p. 57). Clearly, individuals who remain focused and aware while reading will comprehend more of what they read than those who possess less of this quality of mindfulness. One student teacher who was taking a course on deep reading commented,

> Throughout my reflective online journal writing and attempt at deep reading, I was able to reflect and understand my own awareness (or lack of at times) in my own learning. At times it was difficult because I felt as if my mind would constantly wander and I would have to redirect my focus on whatever it was I was reading. Eventually, I felt as if it became easier because I was able to recognize when a distracting thought was developing. (Hall, O'Hare, Santavicca, & Jones, 2015, p. 52)

Studies are beginning to demonstrate that mindfulness as a practice, even apart from deep reading, results in increased reading comprehension (see, e.g., Clinton, Swenseth, & Carlson, 2018; Tarrasch, Berman, & Friedmann, 2016).

Here are other practical strategies teachers can use to integrate mindfulness into their reading, literature, and ELA programs.

- *Choose books that illustrate themes that are relevant to mindfulness.* The children's book *Alexander and the Terrible, Horrible, No Good, Very Bad Day* by Judith Viorst, for example, provides a way of talking about events in students' lives that unsettle the mind and that require a mindful attitude (see Appendix B for a list of children's literature selections that directly focus on mindfulness). At the high school level, students might read selections from Henry David Thoreau's book *Walden,* and in particular those passages in which he talks about being mindful regarding nature. After reading the text, students can take a walk outdoors and use their mindfulness skills to be aware of the sights, sounds, tastes, smells, and textures around them.
- *Study poems that reflect a mindful attitude.* Japanese poetry—haiku, in particular—has deeper meaning when approached from the point of view of each "present moment" in nature, and students can be encouraged to write their own mindful haiku after taking a walk outside.
- *Learn about the inner worlds of characters in the novels, stories, and poems studied in the curriculum.* One high school assignment for studying William Shakespeare's play *Romeo and Juliet* might be to write an essay on the question of how Romeo and Juliet's fate might have been different if they'd taken a course on mindfulness. Or a class might study the stream-of-consciousness writing method employed by James Joyce in his novel *Ulysses,* in which the entire last chapter is nothing but the inner thoughts of one of its chief characters, Molly Bloom, as she drifts off to sleep.
- *Examine famous quotations from literature and discuss their meaning in terms of mindfulness practice.* The English poet Milton, for example, included the following line in his epic poem *Paradise Lost*:

"The mind is its own place, and in itself, can make a Heav'n of Hell, a Hell of Heav'n." Students can be encouraged to share instances in their own lives of when this line seemed particularly apt. For younger students, a quote from Winnie the Pooh might be a good starter for discussion or writing, "People say nothing is impossible, but I do nothing every day."

• *Use metaphor in literature as a stepping-off point for under-standing mindfulness.* For example, as part of a mindfulness program called iRest for Kids (see Appendix B for contact information), students read the Hans Christian Andersen fairy tale *The Princess and the Pea.* Afterward, they lay on the floor while the teacher placed a single pea in the palm of each student's hand. She then asked if they could be as sensitive to their pea as the princess was to hers and explored the different sensory attributes of the pea (Shapiro et al., 2015).

Mindful Writing as a Core Literacy Activity

Although teaching writing involves formal skills such as grammar, spelling, and sentence structure, another major component deals with connecting the experience of the writer to the words that appear on the page. Mindful writing is an excellent strategy for making those connections. As with reading, in mindful writing we substitute the act of writing for the breath, focusing all our attention on what we're writing, and if we find our mind wandering, noticing the digression and returning to the task at hand. The only difference from formal mindfulness practice is that our wandering mind may often pick up new ideas, associations, and memories that we can incorporate into our writing.

Ted Curtin (2017), an 8th grade teacher at the Waldorf School in Cape Cod, Massachusetts, uses walks in nature as a way of sparking mindful moments that can be recorded in writing:

> When we return to the classroom from our morning walk, we sometimes take a few minutes to write something about some aspect of the morning that has touched our thoughts or feelings, or that we have purposefully focused our attention on. Last week, on a morning misted with a light rain, we stopped in at the Sunhouse [the school's

greenhouse]. We sat quietly and took in the experience of the place and the moment and then went in to write some impressions. As usual, there were many examples from the students of perceptive observation and beautiful description, in poetry and prose.

Here are some other ways to link mindfulness to writing activities:

• *Have students create their own mindfulness scripts or exercises,* which they can then record and use at home to guide their mindfulness practice.

• *Use the writing prompt "I am aware . . ."* to stimulate student writing on present-moment experiences.

• *Ask students to write down the ideas running through their minds (stream of consciousness) as they experience them.* This is a good way to break through writer's block and lets students externalize their mind wandering—making it easier to notice during their formal mindfulness practice.

• *Have students take their stream of consciousness assignments* and turn them into finished writing projects (e.g., a radio play, a video presentation, a blog post).

• *Let students keep mindfulness journals,* where they write down their day-to-day experience of practicing mindfulness. Even two minutes of journaling time per day is often adequate for most kids to process their mindfulness activities.

Being Mindful with Math

Mathematics for many students is primarily about learning algorithms and then solving an endless sequence of problems in preparation for high-stakes tests. The idea of just "sitting" with a math problem seems alien to this way of learning. Yet a certain degree of mindfulness may actually promote greater engagement (and even accuracy) with the material. Here's how high school math teacher and mindfulness instructor Richard Brady (2005) counseled one of his algebra students in mindful math:

> Last spring I advised an algebra student to slow down and just to do the math, not to try to get it finished in order to go on to the next

thing. Intellectually she understood what I was saying. She wanted to follow my advice, but her habit of rushing was very strong, so she kept doing her work in the same way.... When my students encounter obstacles, their first impulse is usually towards one of two extremes: they try to overcome them or they give up. The approach of welcoming obstacles, sitting with them, and seeing what gifts of understanding they have to offer is foreign to my students, yet it is one that could serve them well in life.

Here are some ways to bring mindfulness into the math experience of your students:

• *Suggest to students that they do a "mindful math problem"* in which they focus all their attention on the problem, notice any mind wandering, and then return their attention to the problem. Ask them if this makes the problem easier to complete or more enjoyable to work on.

• *Use mindful stretching poses to study symmetry* (e.g., which poses are symmetrical, what lines of symmetry exist, what effect do changes in the poses have on symmetry?).

• *Have students keep track of the number of normal breaths they take* during a mindfulness session and then graph the results for the whole class.

• *Let students keep a math log* in which they record their mindful experiences in math class (e.g., encountering aha moments or a "math block" [akin to a writer's block]).

Mindfulness in Learning Science

Keen observation ability is one of the most important attributes of a good scientist. There's a legendary story about the biologist Louis Agassiz asking one of his students to describe a sunfish specimen that was on view in their laboratory. He left the room for a few minutes, came back, and the student gave his observations. "Keep looking," Agassiz told him and left the lab for several hours. In the interim, the student saw many more things. "Great! Keep looking!" said the famous scientist on his return, and then left the lab for several days. Finally, when Agassiz returned, the student knew something about the sunfish. Essentially, this attitude toward patient observation is similar to the concept of mindfulness and can be used effectively in the science classroom. One 5th grade teacher had his students learn about Earth's atmosphere by taking them outside and having them lie on their backs and look up at the sky. He then said to them,

> Can you see those treetops over there? Can you see those birds flying above the trees? Can you see those low puffy clouds? Can you see above those clouds to the thin wispy ones beyond? There's depth to the sky—some things in the sky are higher than others. That's because the sky is actually like an ocean of air. (Girod, Twyman, & Wojcikiewicz, 2010, p. 811)

Here are some other ways to inject mindfulness into your science lessons:

• *Take your students on a mindful safari.* Go outdoors to look at flowers and plants (botany), animals (zoology), or insects (entomology) and really focus in depth on individual specimens using the senses of touch, smell, sight, and hearing. Back in the classroom, have students write about or draw their favorite specimens in their own naturalist's field guide.

• *Investigate the science of breathing,* including how the lungs work, the diffusion of oxygen throughout the blood stream, and other physiological and anatomical features that are critical to respiration.

• *Study the science of stress,* including the HPA axis and SAM axis (as described in Chapter 2), the evolutionary function of stress, the importance of stress reduction, and how to manage a lifestyle that minimizes the negative effects of stress.

• *Learn about how the brain works,* including key areas involved in processing the stress response and structural and functional changes that occur in the brain as a result of mindfulness practice.

• *Use mindful stretching poses to teach about the natural world.* For example, one trainer reported how he used poses to emulate a river experience in the classroom:

We went to a river: the pose we used was forward bend, but I called it something different in order to make it fit the story, so a forward bend became the flowing river as we reached up and folded over at the hip joint. Then we got into our kayaks by doing boat pose, sitting on our bums with our arms and legs in a V, a balancing pose. We followed with a variety of other poses which represented birds, the waves of the ocean, fish, whales, and dolphins. (Thomas, 2008)

• *Investigate the physics of mindful stretching poses.* One writer, for example, explains the "bow" pose (lying on one's belly and lifting up the head while simultaneously raising the legs off the floor and reaching back to hold onto them):

[The pose] involves perpetual pendulum-like back and forth swings performed with agility and grace. Beginners confuse it with strength training and try to lift both the ends simultaneously. I remind my friends of Newtonian [p]hysics. Let the pelvic bone act as a pivot and gently use the weight of the head to gather momentum and steer. And the swing is established thanks to [i]nertia of [m]otion. Once the extreme swing is reached, the body obeys Galilean [relativity] and oscillates back to the opposite side establishing a near perpetual motion. (Ratnala, 2018)

Mindful History and Social Studies

History and social studies are largely about people, and thus they offer the opportunity to learn about people's beliefs, motivations, aspirations, and other dimensions of their inner life. For example, while watching televised presidential debates, one 8th grader remarked that the two candidates weren't exactly listening to each other. What effect would kindness and compassion have on the political scene? How would history have been different if the major players had been more mindful? These are the types of questions that are worth pursuing in conjunction with mindful practice. Here are some specific examples of how this might work:

• *Raise thoughtful questions on topics of current interest.* On the topic of health care in the United States, for example, ask, "Is there a moral imperative for a government to provide health care for all of its citizens?" "What do the examples of health care in different countries around the world tell us about the need for compassion and kindness in looking after a country's elders?"

• *Have students study a great figure from world history* (e.g., Napoleon, Alexander the Great, Pericles) and investigate the extent to which that individual exhibited characteristics of mindfulness versus mindlessness in beliefs or actions.

• *Study a major conflict from U.S. history or world history* (e.g., the Civil War, World War II) and have students write an essay on how mindfulness exercised by one or more of the major players might have altered the course of events.

• *Discuss the question "What are some ways in which a community might demonstrate mindfulness or kindness and compassion in helping its local inhabitants?"* Follow up with questions such as these: "To what extent does your own community display these traits?" "How might it improve in its ability to help others?"

Mindfulness in the Arts

Perhaps no other subject in school better reflects the principles of mindfulness than the arts (painting, sculpture, music, drama). In a very real sense, the creative act is indistinguishable from a mindful attitude. Here is how one artist expresses this sensibility:

> [A]fter a few minutes of actually paying attention to the feel of the brush on the canvas, the smell of paint, the sound of the palette knife scraping as I mixed and blended colours together in pursuit of the perfect blue or red, something would shift. The classroom would fall away. It was just me and my paintbrush. I *was* the paintbrush—we moved in unison. I felt the rough canvas underneath me, the cool sensation of being dipped in paint, the warm breath, as I leaned closer and closer to the canvas, paying attention to some detail. (Constantinescu, 2012)

In her best-selling book *Drawing on the Right Side of the Brain*, author Betty Edwards (2012) counsels the reader to draw what he directly *sees* rather than some mental image of what the subject looks like. This mindful attitude has much in common with the concept of flow developed by psychologist Mihaly Csikszentmihalyi (2008), which he conceived while studying artists and other highly proficient individuals. Whether studying the creative work of geniuses or practicing one or more of the arts on one's own, this quality of staying in the present moment is critical to any truly creative work of art.

Here are several ways to maintain a mindful attitude in students while they are engaged in the creative arts or studying the history of art, music, drama, or allied disciplines:

• *Visual arts*—Have them select an object, look carefully at it for a few minutes, and then draw exactly what they see in front of them, line by line.

• *Music history*—Engage them in mindful music appreciation by setting aside time to listen to specific pieces of music in a genre (e.g., classical, jazz, blues). In this case, the music becomes the breath that they focus their attention on, and when their minds wander, suggest that they gently redirect their attention to the music.

• *Dance*—Have them choreograph a dance that includes mindful stretching poses as a part of the total work.

• *Dramatic arts*—Ask them to practice "becoming one" with a character in a play, experiencing that character's actions moment by moment.

As you can see from the wide range of activities described in this chapter, mindfulness needn't be restricted to formal practices such as breathing, walking, or eating. The whole curriculum is available as a template for mindful activities. By weaving mindfulness into the whole school day, you'll be reinforcing the practices themselves and delivering an important message to students that learning is about staying in the present moment and being OK with whatever emerges in the process.

Takeaways

• Some educators are concerned that mindfulness activities will take time away from academics, but mindfulness supports academic achievement in several ways, including helping students refocus their attention on learning material at the start of a new class, assisting students in overcoming math anxiety, developing cognitive functions like working memory that are essential to academic success, and being integrated as content directly into the curriculum.

• Mindful reading involves focusing the mind on the text and noticing when and where the mind wanders. Mindful reading strategies include choosing literature that reflects mindful principles, studying poems that reflect awareness of the present moment, and reflecting on the *mindfulness* versus *mindlessness* of key characters in novels, plays, or short stories.

• Mindful writing is similar to mindful reading in that the practitioner makes the text the central focus of awareness. Strategies for developing mindfulness in writing include creating mindfulness scripts or exercises, using the writing prompt "I am aware . . . ," and writing haiku that record present moments in nature.

• Mindful math involves slowing down the process of problem solving and simply being with the problem, noticing obstacles, and being open to new insights. Other ways to integrate mindfulness into math include studying the symmetry in mindful stretching poses, keeping a math log of mindful moments, and creating a whole-class chart of the number of breaths per minute individual students take during a mindfulness session.

• Mindful science is linked to the careful observational skills of the scientist. Students can exercise this function by observing different facets of nature (e.g., botany, zoology, and entomology). Other ways of integrating mindfulness into science topics include studying the science of the respiratory system, the science of stress, and the structure and function of different brain regions.

• Mindful history and social science involve the mindfulness (or lack of mindfulness) of people in history, contemporary politics, and the local community. Examples of activities include thinking about how a mindful leader might have altered the course of history or how compassion might influence a country's health care policy.

• Mindful art is related to the close identification of the artist with the object of creation. Examples include drawing exactly what one sees in the external world, listening mindfully to different genres of music, choreographing a dance made up of mindful stretching poses, and being "in the now" while dramatizing a role in a play.

8

Expanding Schoolwide

Thus far we've been looking at mindfulness in terms of its use in individual classrooms. One important purpose of this book is to help teachers implement the tools of mindfulness regardless of their setting. In this chapter, we'll look at the benefits that come from using mindfulness principles and strategies in a systemic way so that the whole school (and even the whole community) benefits. Implementing a whole-school approach to mindfulness is one of the most important factors in ensuring the sustainability of its practices. As Gail Kipper, principal at Farragut Middle School in Hastings-on-Hudson, New York, puts it:

> As an administrator, you can bring something into the building and say, "Listen, I want everybody to do whatever it is," but then people go into their rooms, close the door . . . they do what they're going to do. . . . [Our mindfulness program] is immersed really throughout the entire fabric of the school. (Wilson, 2018)

What's the Weather Like in Your School?

Ultimately, mindfulness can be an important tool in positively influencing school climate. Federal education policy guidelines encourage educators to consider certain nonacademic measures, including school climate (U.S. Department of Education, 2014). Clinical psychologist

Anthony Quintiliani (2015) writes about the cost of a poor school climate:

> When a school is stress-prone, social-emotional stability is harmed, students do not learn well, and teachers and administrators may move into avoidance behaviors to protect themselves from the highly negative psychological and physical effects of chronic stress. Not many people smile or laugh as norms in such systems. More people are absent due to illness and fatigue, and parents and taxpayers are dissatisfied with outcomes versus costs.

He goes on to suggest that "[r]egular mindfulness practices and skills enhance the ability of an individual to find inner peace and joy. . . . [They] reduce negative thinking, negative emotional reactivity, and thus negative classroom and school climate."

Many schools have discovered skillful ways of using mindfulness to enhance school climate. At Renfrew Community Elementary School in Vancouver, British Colombia, school assemblies kick off with a mindfulness breathing exercise. "There are 415 kids in a gym," says principal Hugh Blackman, "and you can hear a pin drop" (Lunau, 2014). At Kermit McKenzie Intermediate School in Guadalupe, California, students spend five minutes in the morning and five minutes in the afternoon quieting their minds via the instructions of a school counselor who uses the school's intercom system to guide all the students in mindfulness practice (Cone, 2016).

At Southern Elementary School in Lexington, Kentucky, students take part in a Yoga 4 Classroom program in the school's library. "So if I have a group that maybe comes in a little rowdy," says school librarian Jillian Anderson, "it's a great method for me to use in order to get them to calm down. Maybe they have sat a while after we've read a story or two and then we can get up and do a yoga pose and it's controlled, but they also get to get up and move" (Philpott, 2018). At Carbondale Community School in Carbondale, Colorado, students kick off "Mindful Mondays" by forming a circle in the commons area for a few minutes of guided mindfulness practice, with time also to discuss real-life instances when mindfulness came in handy (Schimke, 2016). On Mondays at West Milwaukee School in Milwaukee, Wisconsin, students wear special mindfulness T-shirts that say "Keep Calm and Breathe On." A hall exhibit displays art and writing from a 7th grade language arts class on how mindfulness helps them (Borsuk, 2015).

Making Space to Be Mindful

One practical way that mindfulness has been implemented on a school-wide basis is through the use of special areas in the school building where the focus is on helping students gain or regain calm and concentration through mindfulness practices. Concern about the overuse of suspensions and expulsions in schools, particularly as it disproportionately affects students of color, has led administrators to seek alternatives to exclusionary discipline procedures (Sparks & Klein, 2018).

Mindfulness practices represent one important way for students to remain in school and manage their emotions safely. In many cases, a "clam down" space is situated inside individual classrooms. But in other instances, larger areas are set aside for this purpose. Robert W. Coleman Elementary School in Baltimore, Maryland, for example, has a "Mindful Me" room as part of its schoolwide Mindful Moments program. When students enter the room, either after a classroom incident or when seeking help in calming down, a mindfulness practitioner talks to the student about the triggering situation and then guides the student through a mindfulness practice such as breathing exercises or mindful stretching poses. One enraged student who'd been made fun of by another student and ended up in a fight entered the Mindful Me room and later commented, "I did some deep breathing, had a little snack, and I got myself together. . . . Then I apologized to my class" (Bloom, 2016). Asked whether she's noticed suspension cases reduced as a result of the program, principal Carlillian Thompson replied, "We've had zero suspensions" (CBS News, 2016).

These special spaces, which have been given different names by different schools (e.g., Chill Out Zone, Zen Room, Mindfulness Room), aren't just an alternative to discipline. The mindfulness room at the Edgar L. Miller Elementary School in Merrillville, Indiana, is open at-will for any class from kindergarten to 4th grade, as well as for teachers and individual students (Colias-Pete, 2018). Lafayette Elementary

School in Washington, D.C., has an alternate space available for recess and lunch period called the Peace Club, where kids can go to decompress (Ryden, 2018). And Olin Levitt, the psychologist at West Jordan Middle School in Jordan, Utah, has turned his office into a yoga studio to help stressed kids cope (Rascon, 2017). Other schools have situated "quiet zones" in less traveled hallways, libraries, study halls, and garden spaces in the schoolyard.

Another way in which mindfulness can be implemented on a schoolwide basis is by integrating it into existing courses and school programs. Alan Brown, dean of Grace Church School in New York City, has brought mindfulness into his school on multiple levels, including a semester-long elective for 10th through 12th graders that meets an academic requirement; an intensive eight-week course; a mindful movement class; and even parent workshops (Gerszberg, 2018). Students in Mt. Lebanon High School in Pittsburgh, Pennsylvania, do mindfulness activities via an elective in social psychology in which they also keep journals of their experience, learn the brain science that underlies mindfulness practice, and develop habits conducive to well-being (Daly, 2017).

John Adams Middle School in Santa Monica, California, offers 13 hours of training in mindfulness and other components of social and emotional learning throughout the year as part of its physical education program (Pinsker, 2015). East Leyden High School in Franklin Park, Illinois, has a mindfulness club and teaches relaxation techniques as a part of the summer advanced placement program, as an adjunct to its after-school tutoring, and through 9th grade mentoring at the school (Zalaznick, 2017). One recent study suggests that mindfulness activities can be successfully integrated into schools' health education courses to promote healthy behaviors in adolescents (Salmoirago-Blotcher et al., 2018; see also Albrecht, 2014).

The Special Value of a Mindful School Leader

The richness and depth of these programs doesn't appear out of thin air. Among other things, schoolwide mindfulness requires a principal or other school leader who can mobilize the troops and create a mindfulness campaign that touches everyone in the school. This effort requires a special kind of leadership that, not surprisingly, is called "mindful leadership" (see Figure 8.1). Just as teachers need to practice mindfulness before teaching it (see Chapter 4), so, too, do principals and other school leaders (including those at the district level).

Not surprisingly, school leaders report high levels of stress. In one Midwestern study, principals reported personal stress as the leading contributor to the tension in their jobs followed by diminished resources at their schools. They also reported high scores in "insufficient time to get the job done, constant interruptions, loss of personal time, keeping up with e-mail communications, job expectations of the principal, and work-life balance" (cited in Wells, 2015, p. 3). School leaders often have to deal with long hours, pressures to close the achievement gap, and expectations to transform outdated infrastructure. Moreover, they're provided with little to no time to reflect and focus on the complexities of their work responsibilities. School leaders

Figure 8.1

Key Attributes of Mindful School Leaders

A mindful leader
— Inspires hope in others.
— Offers compassion to all.
— Permits freedom to take risks.
— Views mistakes as opportunities to learn.
— Builds a culture of trust with school members.
— Listens deeply to others.
— Communicates in the moment.
— Reacts calmly and rationally to unexpected events.
— Demonstrates emotional intelligence.
— Uses strategies to reduce stress in self and others.
— Shows resilience when negative events occur.
— Has a great sense of empathy.
— Serves as a center of calm in the midst of the storm.
— Takes a genuine interest in what others say and do.
— Possesses a solid understanding of the neuroscience of mindfulness.
— Cultivates a safe work environment.

who experience high enough levels of stress are likely to have a role in creating a poor and even toxic school climate, with teachers reluctant to share what's important to them, kids scared to approach the principal's office, and school personnel unclear about what's expected of them.

The mindful school leader, by contrast, creates a school climate in which teachers aren't afraid of making mistakes, feel listened to, and feel they have permission to experiment in their classrooms. This kind of positive school climate engenders a feeling of mutual trust among all shareholders. Valerie Brown, president of Lead Smart Coaching, which focuses on training school leaders in mindfulness practices and principles, says,

> Mindfulness improves a school leader's ability to notice and to focus, slow down, stop, pause, breathe, and avoid automatic reactions that . . . might later cause regret. The capacity to focus in the moment is a hallmark of leadership excellence. Connecting with others, taking a genuine interest in the well-being of another, listening for what is said and what is left unsaid, supports true understanding and promotes a trustworthy school community. This strengthens the leader's capacity to influence others in a positive way. (DeWitt, 2016)

Lisa Gonzales, president of the Association of California School Administrators and assistant superintendent of educational services at Dublin Unified School District in California, speaks to administrators when she writes:

> Have you ever walked across campus after school hours, deep in thought while mentally preparing your "to-do list," only to have your thoughts interrupted by a parent or staff member? It's hard to be entirely present in the conversation they are pulling you into because your mind is stuck on the list. The task at hand should be the other person, but our brains are often a little scattered with so much work and so little time that we can't focus on that conversation as fully as we would like. That's where mindfulness comes in, as it helps us reconnect with others in a more meaningful, authentic way. (Gonzalez, 2018)

One important function of a mindful school leader can be to organize a partnership with foundations, universities, local city initiatives, or other institutions that can provide the funding, training, and support needed to make schoolwide mindfulness a reality (see Figure 8.2). There is no one way of doing this. Schools have creatively put together such partnerships from diverse sources. Here is a list of some of the partnerships that have worked to bring mindfulness into their schools:

- The afterschool mindfulness program at Robert Bruce Elementary in Santa Maria, California, is under the auspices of the Student Nutrition Advisory Council (SNAC) and includes nutrition, physical exercise, mindfulness practice, and yoga.
- Staff and students at Hilltop High School in West Nyack, New York, were introduced to mindfulness when the Rockland BOCES (a regional education services center) received a suicide-prevention grant from the state Mental Health Association.
- Mindfulness meditation programs at Robert W. Coleman Elementary School and Patterson High School in Baltimore, Maryland, are being funded by the nonprofit Holistic Life Foundation, started by two brothers from the Baltimore area.
- Fifteen schools scattered through five boroughs of New York City received a grant of $10,000 each from a comprehensive mental health initiative called Thrive NYC.
- The UCLA CARES Center is implementing the Calm Classroom program in collaboration with the Partnership for Los Angeles Schools.

Building Faculty Buy-in to Mindfulness Practices

Simply coming up with the money and then finding out-of-school trainers to do professional development programs with teachers is not enough to build a well-designed and sustainable mindfulness program. Of paramount importance is teacher buy-in (and as we'll see later in this chapter, parent buy-in as well). Schoolwide mindfulness essentially has to be a grassroots effort that unfolds naturally.

Figure 8.2

Potential Sources of Partnerships, Funding, and Support for Mindfulness Programs

Type of Institution	Examples
University research centers	Center for Healthy Minds, University of Wisconsin–Madison; Curry School of Education, University of Virginia
Private foundations	Holistic Life Foundation
Prevention programs (e.g., drugs, suicide)	Josh Anderson Foundation
Urban initiatives	Thrive NYC
Mental health associations	New York Mental Health Association
Education institutions	U.S. Department of Education; state-based education service centers (e.g., BOCES in New York, ESCs in Texas); state departments of education
Mindfulness training providers	Mindful Schools
Social and Emotional Learning (SEL) training providers	The Collaborative for Academic, Social, and Emotional Learning (CASEL)
Education foundations	Yes for Schools; Santa Monica–Malibu Education Foundation (SMMEF)
Private donations	Anonymous parent donors
Health/wellness/nutrition organizations	Student Nutrition Advisory Council (SNAC)
Insurance companies	Aetna Insurance

In many cases, successful schoolwide mindfulness programs started with one teacher or principal who already had been practicing mindfulness for some time and was excited by the outcomes and wanted to share the experiences with colleagues. At Farragut Middle School in Hastings-on-Hudson, New York, for example, principal Gail Kipper started individually researching mindfulness and taking online courses years ago. When she felt ready, she invited interested staff members into her office for 15-minute sessions in the morning. The group eventually grew so large that they moved the sessions to a conference room. Then in fall 2017, the first mindfulness room in the school was opened with a $1,271 grant from the Hastings Education Foundation. As interest grew, more teachers took mindfulness training courses and slowly began teaching their students during the class day (Wilson, 2018).

Here are other strategies for making sure that the implementation of mindfulness in your school has a positive outcome:

• Make sure that teachers engage in their own mindfulness practice *before* teaching it to their students (see Chapter 4, which focuses on the importance of teacher mindfulness).

• Although you may want to have expert mindfulness trainers demonstrate teaching in the classroom, remember that research on social and emotional learning programs has shown that students benefit most when their classroom teachers are ultimately the program instructors (Durlak, Weissberg, Dymnicki, Taylor, & Schellinger, 2011).

• Emphasize the scientific basis for mindfulness practices. Distribute both popular and scholarly publications on the subject to teachers, post them on bulletin boards, and have them available on faculty tables in the cafeteria (this book is a good place to start).

• Administrators: Do not mandate that all teachers will teach mindfulness in their classrooms by a certain date. Schoolwide mindfulness cannot be forced; top-down programs are likely to burst. Be patient, work slowly, and watch the program grow naturally from educator to educator.

• Formal training programs (such as Mindful Schools or MindUP) can be excellent ways to expose teachers to the ins and outs of mindfulness practice, but the out-of-towners are going to leave eventually so it is essential for teachers to find meaningful ways of bringing mindfulness into their classrooms in a way that reflects each classroom's individuality.

• If you're just getting started, identify a cohort of teachers and staff in your school who have been practicing mindfulness on their own and are excited about the possibilities of bringing it to the school. These individuals can serve as the motivators, cheerleaders, and catalysts to spread interest and enthusiasm to other members of the faculty.

- Locate the naysayers, wet blankets, saboteurs, and hypercritical staff and listen carefully to their objections and concerns. Then address those concerns with good information and modifications in the program as needed.

- For teachers who object that mindfulness is a waste of good instructional time, make sure that they reread the sections of this book that talk about how much time is already wasted by stressed-out kids who can't focus—for example, the first part of Chapter 7, and also the section in Chapter 1 that shows how mindfulness overlaps with many existing educational programs (see Figure 1.1).

- Once teachers are directly leading their students in mindfulness practices, encourage them to be creative so that the practices don't become dull, routine, or doctrinaire. Fifth grade teacher Jim Librandi at Julian Curtiss School in Greenwich, Connecticut, says, "Mindfulness affects each student in a different way. It's like personalized learning, but for social-emotional learning. . . . Eventually the students realized I was making up the exercises. . . . Then they started making up their own exercises and applauding each other" (*Greenwich Free Press*, 2017).

To establish a truly schoolwide, enduring mindfulness campaign, look beyond classrooms, teachers, and students and engage other members of the school and the community as well. Parents should be brought into the program as early as possible, to experience mindfulness personally and to ask questions and share doubts and concerns. For example, some religious parents might be concerned about what they see as an intrusion of spirituality into the school day, in violation of the separation of church and state in public schools. Chapter 9 focuses in detail on this question, but experience has shown that troubles erupt when parents are not informed early on about the program and its secular focus.

Another way to expand mindfulness is by teaching it to the support personnel at your school—the food service crew, the custodial team, and the secretarial pool. The Las Cruces Public Schools offer a wellness program that includes mindfulness practice supported through the New Mexico Public School Insurance Authority (Linan, 2018). This support suggests that insurance companies have a stake in seeing that their customers stay mentally and physically healthy. Here are some other ideas:

• *Form an alliance with a neuropsychologist, a neurologist, a psychologist, or a psychiatrist* who can serve as an advisor to your mindfulness program.

• *Meet with local clergy to allay concerns and potential misunderstandings* regarding the alleged claim that mindfulness is a religious activity (when it is, in fact, a secular program with a strong scientific base). See Chapter 9 for a full discussion of this issue.

• *Ask teachers who have taken mindfulness training programs off campus to share with the staff* what they've learned.

• *Conduct a survey of teachers* to get their opinions about setting up a mindfulness program at your school.

• *Assign an enthusiastic group of faculty or administrators to keep track of program data* (suspensions, expulsions, trips to the principal's office, drop-outs, bullying, grades, test scores, student attitudes toward mindfulness).

• *Consider creating a new staff position at your school: mindfulness specialist.* Fill the role with someone who has considerable personal experience with mindfulness, including mindfulness workshops and at least one teacher-training program from a mindfulness group (see Appendix B for a list of several groups, including contact information).

What's particularly exciting about a schoolwide approach to mindfulness is what can happen when the practices get passed throughout the community in unexpected ways. In Greenwich, Connecticut, for example, a father noticed how his son played differently with his 4-year-old brother and took breaks when appropriate. In addition, students from the local school shared mindfulness techniques with Greenwich first-responders, including the police department, the fire department, and the emergency medical services team. Once the mindfulness genie is out of the bottle, there are no limits to its far-reaching outcomes!

Takeaways

• Although adoption of mindfulness practices by individual classroom teachers is clearly important, mindfulness has greater sustainability when it is implemented schoolwide.

• Schoolwide mindfulness programs can help significantly improve school climate.

• Examples of schoolwide adoption of mindfulness include its use in assemblies, during school announcements on the intercom, during library time, in designated "chill out" spaces in the school, and through different courses and electives in the curriculum such as physical education, psychology class, and health education.

• A key component of a schoolwide mindfulness program is strong mindful leadership that creates an atmosphere in which teachers aren't afraid of making mistakes, feel listened to, and feel permission to experiment in their classrooms.

• Mindfulness programs differ greatly from school to school but develop as a result of unique partnerships among the school and specific mindfulness organizations, foundations, universities, urban initiatives, and/or state and federal agencies.

• A key to a successful schoolwide mindfulness campaign is to enlist teacher buy-in to the program. This buy-in can be accomplished by avoiding a top-down adoption, being patient and letting it unfold naturally, listening and responding to doubters' concerns, tapping the enthusiasm and expertise of teachers experienced in mindfulness practices, and emphasizing the strong scientific basis of mindfulness.

• A successful schoolwide mindfulness program should grow beyond the students, teachers, and administrators, and embrace other school personnel (lunch staff, support personnel, custodial team) and parents. Parents should be informed early about the program, given a chance to experience mindfulness directly, provided with an opportunity to have questions and concerns answered, and given the right to opt out if necessary.

9

Respecting the First Amendment

While doing research for this book, I ran into numerous instances in which, under the guise of mindfulness, children in public schools have engaged in practices that appeared to have had religious or spiritual overtones. In the United States, the Bill of Rights to the Constitution includes a clause in the First Amendment respecting the separation of church and state. Although teachers can teach students *about* different religions, they absolutely cannot involve them in any religious practices per se. So when I see children with their eyes closed in the lotus position and their hands forming *mudras* (hand gestures that have religious significance), I see the First Amendment being violated. When I listen to a teacher who is leading children on a guided visualization that asks them to imagine the God within them, or to visualize a bright light in their heart chakra spreading out to encompass the whole world, I'm seeing the separation of church and state being breached. When I hear teachers say, "Now we're going to do the Dhanurāsana pose" or read of an instructor ending a mindfulness session by having every student press their hands together and say the word *namaste*, then I'm witnessing still other violations of the First Amendment. Parents of different faiths who have witnessed or heard about these practices going on in public schools have been right to raise their voices in indignation. If these practices can go on, why not Bible study and prayer in public school classrooms?

Is Mindfulness "Stealth Buddhism" or "Stealth Health"?

The trouble with these distortions of secular mindfulness is that those who object to some of the practices just mentioned also rail against the *entire* practice of mindfulness as it is responsibly being presented and practiced in the schools. Before we get into this issue, however, let's first lay our cards on the table. The roots of mindfulness are indeed in ancient Buddhism. Chiesa, Serretti, and Jakobsen (2013) write:

> The original term of what is commonly referred to as mindfulness is Sati, a Sanskrit word that has been both used to indicate a lucid awareness of what is occurring within the phenomenological field and as a term that could be translated as "remembrance" . . . mindfulness has traditionally been defined as an understanding of what is occurring before or beyond conceptual and emotional classifications about what is taking or has taken place. . . . Mindfulness has also been defined as a development of one's own memory. . . . This, in turn, is supposed to enhance the ability not to forget the ethical consequences of one's own behaviours and to exploit this increased ability so as to facilitate one's own ethical development, as it is emphasized by traditional mindfulness practices. (p. 84)

Note that this lengthy definition of *mindfulness* contains little that translates into how mindfulness is actually being used and practiced in schools today: to help students focus, self-regulate, be aware, and reduce stress.

The situation is clear: mindfulness as it should be—and usually is—taught in public schools is entirely secular and grounded not in religion, but in science. The bedrock event that serves as a foundation for mindful practices in schools is Jon Kabat-Zinn's development of the Mindfulness-Based Stress Reduction program at the University of Massachusetts Medical School in the early 1970s and the subsequent output of thousands of scientific studies, many of them adhering to the high standard of randomized controlled trials. Mindful practices in schools do not represent what some critics have called "stealth Buddhism," in which simply a few words have been changed (for example, *mindfulness* to replace *meditation*, *stretching* to replace *yoga*) to hide its true intentions.

Some examples might clarify the matter. In the middle ages, choral singing was an important part of religious ceremonies (it still is in many places). Public schools also practice choral singing (even sometimes of religious works), but few people would argue that a school choir represents a violation of church and state. The reason is because the context and the intention are different in the two situations. In medieval times, choral music was a way of glorifying God and a means of testifying to one's faith in the divine. In the modern school, choral singing is an elective or extracurricular activity that serves to develop one's musical capacities and historical knowledge while providing the opportunity to bond with like-minded friends and acquaintances and strengthen school spirit. Another example is the "golden rule" ("Do unto others as you would have them do unto you"), which forms a central part of the ethical basis of several religions. Few would claim that teaching the golden rule to young children violates the separation of church and state.

The key here is context and intention. The context for mindfulness is that it is an evidence-based set of practices with a growing scientific base. The intention is not to glorify God or trick guileless children into Eastern mysticism (and if any public school practitioners have this as a goal, they should stop teaching mindfulness to students immediately). Rather, the intention is to help students deal with crippling levels of societal stress, develop more mature ways of handling their emotions, cultivate the ability to focus on academic work more readily, and learn better ways of getting along with others.

Mindfulness No-Nos

To make sure that mindfulness is taught and practiced in a secular way, it is absolutely imperative that public school teachers develop a sensibility for what is responsible practice and what is irresponsible practice (see Figure 9.1). Teachers' use of a Tibetan singing bowl or Tibetan bells to signal the starting point and ending point of a mindfulness session is inappropriate and should be substituted with secular bells and chimes. The practice of using the original Indian names to describe specific poses (e.g., "Sālamba Sarvāṅgāsana") must end, and secular names should be used instead (animal and plant names—such as "tree pose"—are particularly appropriate, especially for younger children).

Figure 9.1

Do's and Don'ts for Teaching Mindfulness in U.S. Public Schools

Instructional Activity	Do's (Responsible Approach)	Don'ts (Irresponsible Approach)
Signal the time to start and stop mindfulness session.	Use secular chimes, bells, or soothing smartphone tones.	Use Tibetan singing bowl, Tibetan chimes, or other religiously oriented musical instruments.
Name and describe specific mindful stretching poses.	Use secular names (e.g., animals, plants, geological formations).	Use original Sanskrit names for the poses.
Describe the processes of mindful breathing, walking, eating.	Describe them as "mindfulness practices."	Refer to them as "meditations."
Teach students about proper breathing techniques.	Emphasize that all students need to do is breathe normally during mindful breathing sessions, with some deeper breathing in mindful stretching poses.	Teach specialized breathing techniques like alternate-nostril breathing or rapid-fire breathing.
Teach students to be kind to one another.	Use kindness curriculum activities.	Do religiously toned and guided visualization, such as telling students to imagine they all have God within their hearts that unites them in oneness.
Help students relax after recess or lunch.	Conduct a mindful breathing session or progressive body scan.	Lead them on a visualization of the seven chakras in their body or a chant of a sacred syllable such as "om."

continued

Figure 9.1 (continued)

Do's and Don'ts for Teaching Mindfulness in U.S. Public Schools

Instructional Activity	Do's (Responsible Approach)	Don'ts (Irresponsible Approach)
Teach students rituals of kindness and respect for one another.	Suggest that students say and do nice things for each other during the classroom day.	Teach students when greeting each other to press their hands together at the level of their heart, bow, and say "namaste."
Tell students what to do with their hands while they are engaged in mindful breathing.	Suggest that students put their hands on their lap, on their desk— wherever it feels most comfortable.	Teach students special Hindu mudras or hand gestures that have special significance (e.g., "fear dispeller," "boon bestower").

Some people find the word *yoga* suspect. In a court case in Encinitas, California, two parents sought to close down their children's school yoga program. The California appeals court upheld a district court's decision that the yoga program was "devoid of any religious, mystical, or spiritual trappings" that would violate the separation between church and state (Perry, 2015). The word *yoga* as it is used in schools refers to nothing more than certain postures, poses, or movements that students do with mindfulness. The religious meaning of *yoga* is far more complex and involved; Hinduism encompasses numerous kinds of yoga, including *hatha yoga* (physical yoga), *karma yoga* (good deeds yoga), and *bhakti yoga* (devotional yoga). None of these terms or meanings are relevant to school use and teachers should be careful when teaching (and naming) the poses to avoid any special spiritual or religious meanings that are associated with them. (If teaching a course in Asian history, however, this information could be safely imparted if not accompanied by the practice of the poses.)

The basic orientation in teaching mindfulness is to err on the side of the secular. Doing so may prove difficult for teachers or administrators who are practicing Buddhists and want to impart through stories, quotations, posters, and songs the ideals that have inspired them. But we have to realize that public schools in the United States have had many more Christian educators who have had the same longing to impart biblical truths to students but have had to inhibit that desire because of the constitutional issues. There can't be two (or more) standards, with one group imparting religious beliefs while another is explicitly prevented from doing so.[1]

Parents as Powerful Partners

An important step to take to avoid faith-based misunderstandings is to make sure that parents know about a mindfulness program as soon as it's up and running. One suggestion is to conduct a back-to-school night during which parents learn about the scientific basis for mindfulness, experience a taste of mindfulness practice, and then have the opportunity to ask questions about how it works in the classroom.

Warstler Elementary School in Plain Township, Ohio, stopped its mindfulness program after parents and community members complained that it was too much like practicing Eastern religions such as Buddhism. The program was shut down despite being credited for boosting the school's performance index on state report cards. Previous performance had been stagnant for years. Melanie Snedeker, vice president of the Warstler parent-teacher organization, was among those parents who had concerns about mindfulness. She didn't think the district did a good enough job explaining mindfulness and what it involved to parents. "Once I started talking to parents, they had no clue this was going on," she said. "As soon as it comes out that there's a new website we will do for math, they [the district] are all over it. When it came to mindfulness, they kept their mouths shut. Why the lack of communication if it is so awesome?" (Warsmith, 2013). Buckingham Elementary School in Berlin, Maryland, dealt with parental concerns quite differently. "In Worcester County public schools, we value the partnerships we have with our parents, their families and the Worcester County community as a whole, which includes our faith-based partners," said Carrie Steers, the district coordinator of public relations and special programs. "As we do with any concerns raised from these partners, we invited those individuals with questions about

---

[1] I have deliberately chosen to omit references a popular contemplative school program called Quiet Time because it is based on the use of transcendental meditation, which is explicitly rooted in the teachings of Maharishi Mahesh Yogi (Yogi, 2001).

the program to come in and observe firsthand Mindfulness Moments at Buckingham Elementary School. After the group's observation it was expressed that there were no further concerns, and no programmatic changes have been made." Steers confirmed that the school has changed the word *yoga* to *stretching* but said that's the only change (Parker, 2018).

Clearing Up a Few Misconceptions

Here are a few misconceptions that parents and others in the community may have about mindfulness practices, followed by some clarifications:

• **Claim:** "Mindfulness is just another form of mind control over our children."

Clarification: Mindfulness actually helps children *gain control of their own minds* so that they're not subject to the vagaries of destructive thoughts, feelings, and moods.

• **Claim:** "Mindful meditation involves breathing in a certain way."

Clarification: Students are told to breathe in their normal rhythm and simply be aware of their inhalations and exhalations.

• **Claim:** "Breathing in this way brings one into an altered state where critical thinking and judgment are suspended."

Clarification: Mindful breathing helps students to become aware of their critical thinking and judgments and to examine them with curiosity and see how they affect their lives.

• **Claim:** "Mindfulness as taught in schools is communicating to a child that he should always be calm, always clear-headed, always in control. This certainly could convey a negative message to more emotional children and to children with various psychological, neurological, and emotional problems, as well as making them self-conscious about their feelings."

Clarification: Mindfulness doesn't aim to make students feel calm, clear-headed, and always in control; in fact, it helps them become aware that these qualities are transient. Students who are more emotional are helped by gaining greater self-regulation over their feelings, and students with other problems, who are already self-conscious about their feelings, learn to approach them with a nonjudgmental and curious attitude.

- **Claim:** "Guided visualization is a form of hypnosis, which should cause alarm, if indeed this form of visualization is being used."

Clarification: Mindfulness practices do not use guided visualizations or any methods associated with hypnotism. The emphasis is on students making individual discoveries about how their thoughts, feelings, sensations, and perceptions come and go over time and don't have to rule their lives.

- **Claim (regarding yoga):** "There are spirits invited in by focusing on things not of God; there is an unholy spirit behind it."

Clarification: This claim is a theological belief that cannot be either proven or denied through rational scientific investigation. Virtually all of what secular schools focus on—for example, history, science, literature, math—is "not of God." Would that mean that these subjects are also entangled with unholy spirits?

- **Claim:** "The scientific research on mindfulness in the schools is still in its infancy, and not all studies have shown unequivocal gains. So are we not rushing too quickly into widespread implementation of its practices?"

Clarification: It's true that research on mindfulness in education is still in its early days. Many studies have shown only small to moderate positive effect sizes, and a few have demonstrated no effect at all (see, e.g., Johnson, Burke, Brinkman, & Wade, 2016). But a preponderance of evidence suggests that this is an intervention that has empirical support and should be studied further and applied to school populations so that its effects can be better examined.

I want to reiterate my concern that religious or spiritual practices may have found their way into the mindfulness movement in some schools. My worry is that this will engender an understandable backlash from parents, who will see religion being imported into the schools. I fear the emergence of a Supreme Court case in which the irresponsible use of some of these methods is going to be judged unconstitutional and educators will then become overly cautious, mindfulness practices will get caught up in the subsequent firestorm, and mindfulness will become the latest educational fad to hit the dust. This possibility is why it's particularly important for educators to practice mindfulness correctly in the public schools—in a totally secular way, with no fancy hand gestures, yogic postures, Hindu and Buddhist terminology, Tibetan singing bells, affirmations, visualizations, or sermons.

Takeaways

• Although mindfulness has its roots in ancient Buddhist tradition, it has been entirely secularized as an evidence-based set of practices with a sound scientific foundation.

• Despite the fact that mindfulness is for the most part being taught in the schools in an entirely responsible and secular manner, in some public schools the trappings of Buddhism and other religions have been intentionally or unintentionally incorporated into those practices. To ensure the viability of the model, these irresponsible practices must stop so that they don't endanger the sustainability of the entire movement.

• Examples of irresponsible activities in mindfulness practice in U.S. public schools include the use of hand *mudras* (positions of the hands having spiritual connotations), religious instruments (e.g., Tibetan singing bowls and bells), spiritual terms (e.g., the word *namaste* as a salutation, the name Sālamba Sarvāṅgāsana to describe a yoga pose), religious concepts ("we are all one in the spirit"), and spiritual practices (e.g., alternate nostril breathing and "fire breathing").

• Educators using mindfulness in the schools should err on the side of secularity when there is any doubt about the suitability of any practice or activity.

• Parents should be involved as early as possible in the implementation of a mindfulness program in the school. They should be informed of the program, have a chance to experience mindfulness directly, and have their questions and concerns answered so that misconceptions about mindfulness are cleared up. Experience has shown that this partnership approach to mindfulness reduces the chances of parental disapproval of the program or its practices.

10

Anticipating Future Challenges

A news story picked up by *The New York Times* illustrates possible future challenges that might affect mindfulness in the schools. At a Success Academy charter school in Brooklyn, a group of 1st graders were sitting in a circle doing a math lesson. One of the students, a girl, was asked to explain how she solved a certain math problem, but she got confused. As the newspaper reports:

> She begins to count: "One . . . two. . . ." Then she pauses and looks at the teacher. The teacher takes the girl's paper and rips it in half. *"Go to the calm-down chair and sit,"* she orders the girl, her voice rising sharply. "There's nothing that infuriates me more than when you don't do what's on your paper," she says, as the girl retreats. (Taylor, 2016, italics added)

A video camera caught the whole interaction on tape. There are clearly several problems with the way the teacher responded, but what is salient here is that a "calm-down chair" was used as a punishment for not meeting an academic goal. Success Academy charter schools have been renowned for their high academic and behavioral standards at the cost of human values (Mead, 2017). In a sense, these schools are a symbol of what our schools have become in the past two decades of educational "reform," with institutions bent on achieving high scores on standardized tests and proficiency with a standardized curriculum.

What is troubling here is that mindfulness-related strategies may be used as "stealth" classroom-control measures to ensure an efficient running of a system that itself badly needs reforming. Success Academy founder Eva Moskowitz has been quoted as saying, "Sometimes when kids look like they're daydreaming, it's because they are, and we can't allow that possibility" (Mead, 2017).

The problem is not restricted to high-performing academies. One teacher training institution's blog makes the following recommendation to teachers:

> Tell [students] that together you are going to start a new stillness challenge and each day you'll see how long it can go. Track your meditation progress on a poster. The object of the challenge? To keep your eyes closed, sit in stillness and . . . focus on breathing slowly. Encourage students to avoid talking and fidgeting. (Room 241 Team, 2018)

At New York City's Brooklyn Urban Garden School, students practice a contemplative method called Quiet Time (based on transcendental meditation) and actually have their performance graded on a scale of zero to two (a two means the student sits alert for most of the time, a one means the student's eyes are open or head is down, and a zero is for a disturbance). Students' average scores are converted to grades that go on their report cards (Kaleem, 2017). At David Crockett Elementary School in Phoenix, Arizona, students are encouraged to practice mindfulness during recess and lunchtime. The school staff places red cups on lunch tables until the students begin to calm down, at which time yellow cups are substituted. But if students at a table begin to get rowdy again, the red cups go back on the table (Gomstyn, 2018).

Even when the implementation of so-called mindfulness strategies is not as egregious as suggested in these examples, some social activists and educators are concerned that mindfulness may serve as a way of placing the responsibility for societal ills on individual students and not on the broader culture. With mindfulness, students are told to accept their anger rather than turn it toward solving social ills such as unsafe neighborhoods, racial disparities, and economic inequity. Similarly, we give students strategies for reducing stress but do little to undo the high-stress learning climate resulting from the increased focus on accountability and testing. University professor and critical theorist David Forbes (2015) points out that "[t]he constant pressure in schools on children to achieve, compete and produce—and at a younger age—leads to stressful feelings and negative consequences for children and teachers. Educators serve up mindfulness as the lubricant that makes the gears run more smoothly." Educator Nancy Bailey (2015) writes: "Using mindfulness to teach young children to respect one another is mostly useless if you never let them play and socialize. It makes no sense to steal a child's recess and then teach them self-control."

Similarly, teacher stress and its amelioration through mindfulness tends to be localized within the individual educator instead of where it should be—in improving working conditions, providing more administrative support, expanding opportunities for collegiality, and giving teachers more control over their teaching. Forbes (2015) argues that mindfulness should become part of a critical pedagogy that

> questions and challenges the policies and conditions that create [teachers'] stress and unhappiness. . . . Public education needs a progressive, integral mindfulness that is also mindful, or critically conscious, of its own position within education and society. This approach to mindfulness connects unreflective personal experience with an informed awareness of one's actual social relations; it connects private troubles with public issues. It interrogates and challenges individualism, the myth of an unchanging, separate self, and points up the evidence for our interdependence with all beings and with the earth itself.

Such a critical pedagogy is, in fact, in harmony with the essential nature of mindfulness practice when it is linked to compassion and kindness (see Chapter 5). When students engage in kindness practices that wish health, prosperity, and peace to ever-widening circles of people (classroom, school, community, nation, planet), they are building an emotional foundation for random acts of kindness, volunteerism, and social activism that can make real these inner intentions.

One of the challenges of mindfulness is to implement a more substantial social-action component to go along with its more inner-directed practices. This challenge is particularly crucial when mindfulness is applied to students of color in high-poverty areas. Some critics have noted that in many schools the practice of mindfulness represents an Asian tradition that's been imposed upon Hispanic and African American students by Caucasian teachers (e.g., Hsu, 2016). Forbes (2015) points out:

> Alienated inner city children learn to accept their lousy learning conditions and not act out their anger. . . . Instead of linking inner awareness to ethical relationships and the social world, mindfulness becomes a technology for furthering or adjusting students and teachers to the dominant social order.

Clearly, mindfulness as described in this book should not be implemented as an isolated set of practices divorced from the broader issues and agendas of the schools. Mindfulness can and should be integrated into the curriculum through mindful reading, mindful art, mindful math, and other applications (see Chapter 7). It should become an essential part of creating a positive school climate (see Chapter 8). Most important, we need to make sure that we don't use mindfulness as a way of pacifying students and teachers to accept a paper-and-pencil, test-ridden learning environment. We must continue to strive for developmentally appropriate learning settings for children and adolescents, including play in early childhood education and hands-on experiences, experiential learning, apprenticeships, and other progressive approaches in elementary and secondary schools (Armstrong, 2006). As Kelly (2016) and others have pointed out, we need to avoid creating "McMindfulness" experiences for children that turn them into passive consumers of self-help technologies and instead empower them to use their discoveries of self and their expressions of kindness and compassion to transform the world into a more humane place in which to live.

Takeaways

• Mindfulness has sometimes been misused as a method of classroom control in which students are sent to "calm centers" as punishment or have their practices regulated through a behavior modification system. These approaches are clearly distortions of true mindfulness activities.

• Some critical educators are concerned that mindfulness may be a tool for subduing students and teachers into accepting poor learning or teaching conditions or ignoring broader social, racial, and economic inequities. This is a particularly important issue to address with regard to students of color in urban poverty settings.

• A critical approach to mindfulness integrates its contemplative practices with kindness and compassion activities that ultimately translate into social activism, volunteerism, and other constructive ways of solving the ills of society.

Appendix A: Glossary of Neuroscience Terms

Allostatic load—the cumulative effects of chronic stress on the body

Amygdala—an almond-shaped structure, made of gray matter, that is part of the limbic system or "emotional brain" and is involved in the detection of emotionally arousing stimuli and the triggering of the fight-or-flight stress response

Anterior cingulate cortex—a structure located behind the brain's frontal lobe associated with self-regulation, including the ability to purposefully direct attention and behavior, inhibit inappropriate knee-jerk responses, and deploy flexible processing strategies

Cerebellum (Latin for "little brain")—a structure at the back of the brain that is important for motor control, emotional regulation, language, mental imagery, and learning

Default mode network—a large-scale functional network of interactive but spatially separate brain regions associated with mind wandering, daydreaming, remembering the past, planning for the future, thinking about the self, and thinking about others; operative when the brain is not involved in a specific task; includes the hippocampus, the posterior cingulate gyrus, the angular gyrus, and several other regions of the brain

Dorsolateral prefrontal cortex—one of the most recently evolved regions of the frontal lobes, with a prolonged period of maturity into adulthood; involved in self-regulation functions including selective attention, cognitive flexibility, planning, inhibition, working memory, and abstract reasoning

Dorsomedial prefrontal cortex—a region of the prefrontal cortex that is important in self-monitoring of one's affective state, creating a sense of self or "me-ness," and considering the mental state of others

Functional connectivity—functionally integrated relationships between spatially separate brain regions (as in the **default mode network**)

Hippocampus—a seahorse-shaped structure buried inside the temple on each side of the brain in the limbic system; critically involved in learning and memory processes and in the modulation of emotional control; can be damaged by chronic stress

HPA axis (hypothalamic pituitary adrenal axis)—the body's central stress-response system, where stress signals cause the hypothalamus to secrete corticotropin-releasing hormone (CRH), causing the anterior pituitary gland to secrete adrenocorticotropic hormone (ACTH), which triggers the adrenal cortex to secrete the stress hormone cortisol, which remains in the blood system for hours after the original stressor

Hypothalamus—a region of the forebrain that coordinates the autonomic nervous system and the activity of the pituitary gland, serving to control hunger, thirst, body temperature, and other homeostatic systems; also involved in emotional activity and sleep

Insular cortex, or insula—a region of the brain deep in the cerebral cortex; involved in consciousness and the regulation of emotion and the body's homeostasis; linked to a wide range of functions including compassion, empathy, perception, motor control, and *interoception* (awareness of bodily states such as thirst, hunger, and cold)

Limbic system—also referred to as the emotional brain, a complex system of networks and nerves under the cerebral cortex; involved in a wide range of functions including emotion, behavior, motivation, long-term memory, and olfaction; includes the hippocampus, the hypothalamus, the amygdala, the cingulate gyrus, and several other structural and functional regions

Neuroplasticity—the brain's ability to reorganize itself throughout life in response to injury, disease, environmental stimulation, or other external or internal changes

Parasympathetic nervous system—part of the autonomic nervous system (complementary to the sympathetic nervous system) that serves to conserve energy by slowing down the heart rate, increasing digestive and glandular activity, and relaxing sphincter muscles in the gastrointestinal tract (also called the "rest-and-digest" or "feed-and-breed" system)

Posterior cingulate gyrus—an area around the midline of the brain that is part of the limbic lobe; represents one node in the default mode network and is important for human awareness, episodic memory retrieval, spatial memory, and emotional salience

Prefrontal cortex—the region of the cerebral cortex that covers the front part of the frontal lobe behind the forehead; important for executive functions such as planning, decision making, inhibition, regulating emotions, paying attention, self-monitoring, and social appraisal

SAM axis (sympathomedullary pathway)—the human body's mechanism for handling acute stress (e.g., the fight-or-flight response), in which the hypothalamus activates the sympathetic nervous system, which triggers the adrenal medulla to secrete the hormones adrenaline and noradrenaline, resulting in increased heart rate, decreased digestive activity, increased respiration, and the release of glucose by the liver for access to instant energy

Stress—the body's response to any type of demand or threat

Sympathetic nervous system—part of the autonomic nervous system (complementary to the parasympathetic nervous system) that is activated in response to acute stress, leading to pupil dilation, increased sweating, increased heart rate, increased blood pressure, decreased digestive activity, and other physiological responses also known as the fight-or-flight response

Ventromedial prefrontal cortex—an area of the prefrontal cortex important for the regulation and inhibition of emotional responses, decision making, and self-control

Appendix B: Resources for Mindfulness in Education

In this section, you'll find resources for extending your understanding and practice of mindfulness, both for yourself as a person and for your work as an educator. With the exception of a few yoga books, I've selected mindfulness materials that are entirely secular. These books, audio guides, apps, and training programs are meant to be comprehensive and reflect resources that are current, popular, and user-friendly. I've indicated grade levels for resources that are primarily for children or adolescents.

Apps

These are available for both iOS and Android devices.
Breathe, Think, Do with Sesame Street (Age 4 and up)
Calm (All ages)
DreamyKid by Taylan Wenzel (Age 8 and up)
Headspace (All ages)
Mindfulness for Children by Jannik Holgersen (Age 5 and up)
Smiling Mind (All ages)
Stop, Breathe, & Think (Age 4 and up)

Audio Guides

Mindfulness and the Brain: A Professional Training in the Science and Practice of Meditative Awareness by Jack Kornfield and Daniel Siegel

Mindfulness for Beginners: Reclaiming the Present Moment and Your Life (Book & CD) by Jon Kabat-Zinn

Books for Children

Ahn's Anger by Gail Silver (Preschool–Grade 3)

Breathe and Be: A Book of Mindfulness Poems by Kate Coombs (PreK–Grade 3)

Breathe Like a Bear: 30 Mindful Moments for Kids to Feel Calm and Focused Anytime, Anywhere by Kira Willey (PreK–Grade 3)

Charlotte and the Quiet Place by Deborah Sosin (PreK–Grade 2)

Have You Filled a Bucket Today? A Guide to Daily Happiness for Kids by Carol McCloud (PreK–Grade 4)

I Am Peace: A Book of Mindfulness by Susan Verde (PreK–Grade 3)

The Lemonade Hurricane: A Story of Mindfulness and Meditation by Licia Morelli (PreK–Grade 3)

The Listening Walk by Paul Showers (PreK–Grade 3)

Listening with My Heart: A Story of Kindness and Self-Compassion by Gabi Garcia (Grades 1–3)

Master of Mindfulness: How to Be Your Own Superhero in Times of Stress by Laurie Grossman and Mr. Musumeci's 5th Grade Class (Kindergarten–Grade 5)

Mind Bubbles: Exploring Mindfulness with Kids by Heather Krantz (Preschool–Grade 3)

The Mindful Dragon by Steve Herman (PreK–Grade 3)

Mindful Monkey, Happy Panda by Lauren Alderfer (PreK–Grade 3)

Moody Cow Meditates by Kerry Lee MacLean (PreK and up)

No Ordinary Apple: A Story About Eating Mindfully by Sara Marlowe (PreK–Grade 2)

Peaceful Piggy Meditation by Kerry Lee MacLean (Kindergarten–Grade 3)

Puppy Mind by Andrew Jordan Nance (PreK–Grade 2)

Silence by Lemniscates (PreK–Grade 2)

Sitting Still Like a Frog: Mindfulness Exercises for Kids (and Their Parents) by Eline Snel (includes 60-minute audio CD of exercises read by Myla Kabat-Zinn) (Kindergarten–Grade 7)

Take the Time: Mindfulness for Kids by Maud Roegiers (Grades 1–3)

Books for Children with Special Needs

The Autism Playbook for Teens: Imagination-Based Mindfulness Activities to Calm Yourself, Build Independence, and Connect with Others by Irene McHenry and Carol Moog

Fidget Wisely: 10 Ways to Teach Mindfulness Skills to Kids Who Can't Sit Still: A Book for Parents, Teachers, and Therapists by Kirsten May Keach

Mindfulness for Kids with ADHD: Skills to Help Children Focus, Succeed in School, and Make Friends by Debra Burdick

Mindfulness for Teens with ADHD: A Skill-Building Workbook to Help You Focus and Succeed by Debra Burdick

Self-Regulation and Mindfulness: Over 82 Exercises & Worksheets for Sensory Processing Disorder, ADHD, & Autism Spectrum Disorder by Varleisha Gibbs

Books for Educators

Cultivating Mindfulness in the Classroom by Jeanie M. Iberlin, with Mike Ruyle

Learning to Breathe: A Mindfulness Curriculum for Adolescents to Cultivate Emotion Regulation, Attention, and Performance by Patricia C. Broderick

The Mindful Education Workbook: Lessons for Teaching Mindfulness to Students by Daniel Rechtschaffen

The Mindful School Leader: Practices to Transform Your Leadership and School by Valerie Brown and Kirsten Olson

Mindful Teacher, Mindful School: Improving Wellbeing in Teaching and Learning by Kevin Hawkins

Mindful Teaching and Teaching Mindfulness: A Guide for Anyone Who Teaches Anything by Deborah Schoeberlein David, with Suki Sheth

Mindfulness for Teachers: Simple Skills for Peace and Productivity in the Classroom by Patricia A. Jennings

A Still Quiet Place: A Mindfulness Program for Teaching Children and Adolescents to Ease Stress and Difficult Emotions by Amy Saltzman

The Stress Reduction Workbook for Teens: Mindfulness Skills to Help You Deal with Stress by Gina M. Biegel

Teach, Breathe, Learn: Mindfulness in and out of the Classroom by Meena Srinivasan

The Way of Mindful Education: Cultivating Well-Being in Teachers and Students by Daniel Rechtschaffen

Books for a General Audience

Full Catastrophe Living: Using the Wisdom of Your Body and Mind to Face Stress, Pain, and Illness by Jon Kabat-Zinn

Mindfulness: An Eight-Week Plan for Finding Peace in a Frantic World by Mark Williams and Danny Penman

No Time Like the Present: Finding Freedom, Love, and Joy Right Where You Are by Jack Kornfield

10% Happier: How I Tamed the Voice in My Head, Reduced Stress Without Losing My Edge, and Found Self-Help That Actually Works—A True Story by Dan Harris

Wherever You Go, There You Are: Mindfulness Meditation in Everyday Life by Jon Kabat-Zinn

Mindful Stretching for Children

Best Practices for Yoga in Schools by Traci Childress and Jennifer Cohen Harper (Eds.)

Classroom Yoga Breaks: Brief Exercises to Create Calm by Louise Goldberg

Mindfulness and Yoga in Schools: A Guide for Teachers and Practitioners by Catherine P. Cook-Cottone

Yoga 4 Classrooms Activity Card Deck by Lisa Flynn

Research Centers

Center for Compassion and Altruism Research and Education (CCARE)—Stanford University School of Medicine; Website: http://ccare.stanford.edu/

Center for Healthy Minds—University of Wisconsin–Madison; Website: https://centerhealthyminds.org/

Center for Mindfulness—University of Massachusetts Medical School; E-mail: mindfulness@umassmed.edu; Website: https://www.umassmed.edu/cfm/

Greater Good Science Center—University of California–Berkeley; E-mail: Greater@berkeley.edu; Website: https://greatergood.berkeley.edu/contact

Mindful Awareness Research Center (MARC)—UCLA Semel Institute for Neuroscience and Human Behavior; E-mail: marcinfo@ucla.edu; Website: https://www.uclahealth.org/marc/contact-us

Training Programs for Educators

Cultivating Awareness and Resilience in Education (CARE for Teachers)—Garrison Institute; E-mail: info@garrisoninstitute.org; Website: https://createforeducation.org/care/

Stress Management and Relaxation Techniques (SMART in Education)—via Passageworks, Website: http://passageworks.org/courses/smart-in-education/

Training Programs for Students

Attention Academy (K–Grade 12). Scottsdale Institute for Health and Medicine; E-mail: mindful@cox.net; Website: http://www.stressbeaters .com/mbsr-education/the-attention-academy-program/

Calm Classroom (K–Grade 12). Luster Learning Institute; Website: https:// calmclassroom.com/pages/contact-us

Inner Explorer (PreK–K; Grades 1–5; Grades 6–8). E-mail: info @innerexplorer.org; Website: www.innerexplorer.org

Inner Kids (PreK–Grade 12). Susan Kaiser Greenland; Website: https:// www.susankaisergreenland.com/inner-kids-model/

iRest for Kids (PreK–Grade 12). c/o iRest Institute; Website: https://www. irest.org/contact

Learning to Breathe (L2B) (Middle School and High School); Website: https://learning2breathe.org/contact/

Master Mind (Grades 4–5). Innovative Research and Training; Website: http://irtinc.us/Products/MasterMind.aspx

Mindful Moment (Elementary and High School). Holistic Life Foundation; Contact Form: https://hlfinc.org/contact/; Website: www .hlfinc.org

Mindfulness in Schools Project (Age 7–11; 11–18). E-mail: enquiries @mindfulnessinschools.org; Website: www.mindfulnessinschools.org

Mindful Schools (Grades K–5; Grades 6–12). Contact Form: https:// help.mindfulschools.org/hc/en-us/requests/new; Website: www .mindfulschools.org

MindUP (Grades PreK–2; Grades 3–5; Grades 6–8). Hawn Foundation; E-mail: hello@mindUP.org; Website: www.mindup.org

Moment Program (Grades 6–7). Innovative Research and Training; Website: http://irtinc.us/Products/Moment.aspx

Smiling Mind (Age 6–12). Contact Form: https://www.smilingmind.com .au/contact-us; Website: https://www.smilingmind.com.au

Still Quiet Place (Age 5–18). Contact Form: http://www.stillquietplace.com/contact; Website: www.stillquietplace.com

Wellness Works in Schools (K–Grade 12). E-mail: wynnekinder@gmail.com; Website: http://www.wellnessworksinschools.com/contact.html

Kindness and Compassion Resources

Compassion Games: Survival of the Kindest Interactive website. http://compassiongames.org

Making Friends with Yourself: A Mindful Self-Compassion Program for Teens & Young Adults. University of California–San Diego and University of North Carolina School of Medicine; E-mail: jalhobbs @yahoo.com; Website: https://www.mindfulselfcompassionforteens.com/msc-for-teens

Pets in the Classroom. https://www.petsintheclassroom.org

Self-Compassion and Mindfulness for Teens Card Deck: 54 Exercises and Conversation Starters by Lee-Anne Gray

Self-Compassion for Teens: 129 Activities and Practices to Cultivate Kindness by Lee-Anne Gray

The Self-Compassion Workbook for Teens: Mindfulness and Compassion Skills to Overcome Self-Criticism and Embrace Who You Are by Karen Bluth

References

Abeles, V. (2016, January 2). Is the drive for success making our children sick? *New York Times*. Retrieved from https://www.nytimes.com/2016/01/03/opinion /sunday/is-the-drive-for-success-making-our-children-sick.html?mcubz=1

Ager, K., Albrecht, N. J., & Cohen, M. (2015). Mindfulness in schools research project: Exploring students' perspectives of mindfulness—What are students' perspectives of learning mindfulness practices at school? *Psychology, 6*(7), 896–914.

Agsar, W. J. B. (2018, May 22). How to help your kids practice mindfulness (without making them sit still). *Tricycle*. Retrieved from https://tricycle.org/trikedaily /mindfulness-kids/

Ahn, S., Ames, A. J., & Myers, N. D. (2012, December 1). A review of meta-analyses in education: Methodological strengths and weaknesses. *Review of Educational Research, 82*(4), 436–476.

Albrecht, N. (2014, April). Wellness: A conceptual framework for school-based mindfulness programs. *International Journal of Health, Wellness & Society, 4*(1), 21–36.

Allen, M., Dietz, M., Blair, K. S., van Beek, M., Rees, G., Vestergaard-Poulsen, P., et al. (2012). Cognitive-affective neural plasticity following active-controlled mindfulness intervention. *Journal of Neuroscience, 32*(44), 15601–15610.

American Psychological Association. (2014, February 11). American Psychological Association survey shows teen stress rivals that of adults. Retrieved from http://www.apa.org/news/press/releases/2014/02/teen-stress.aspx

Anana, C. L. (2018, February 7). Educator self-care is social and emotional learning [blog post]. *Homeroom*. Retrieved from https://blog.ed.gov/2018/02/national -school-counseling-week-educator-self-care-social-emotional-learning/

Arens, A. K., & Morin, A. J. S. (2016). Relations between teachers' emotional exhaustion and students' educational outcomes. *Journal of Educational Psychology, 108*(6), 800–813.

Armstrong, T. (2006). *The best schools: How human development research should inform educational practice*. Alexandria, VA: ASCD.

Armstrong, T. (2007, May). The curriculum superhighway. *Educational Leadership, 64*(8), 16–20.

Armstrong, T. (2016). *The power of the adolescent brain: Strategies for teaching middle and high school students*. Alexandria, VA: ASCD.

Aust, J., & Bradshaw, T. (2017). Mindfulness interventions for psychosis: A systematic review of the literature. *Journal of Psychiatric and Mental Health Nursing, 24*(1), 69–83.

Bailey, N. (2015, July 28). Mindfulness training: Help or cover-up in education-reform affected schools? Retrieved from https://nancyebailey.com/2015/07/28 /mindfulness-training-help-or-cover-up-in-education-reform-affected-schools/

Bakosh, L. S., Snow, R. M., Tobias, J. M., Houlihan, J. L., & Barbosa-Leiker, C. (2016). Maximizing mindful learning: Mindful awareness intervention improves elementary school students' quarterly grades. *Mindfulness, 7*(1), 59–67.

Barnes, N., Hattan, P., Black, D. S., & Schuman-Olivier, Z. (2017). An examination of mindfulness-based programs in U.S. medical schools. *Mindfulness, 8*(2), 489–494.

Bassett, K. (2018, January 3). Bringing a "mindful" presence to the classroom. *Harbor Light*. Retrieved from https://www.harborlightnews.com/articles/bringing-a -mindful-presence-to-the-classroom/

Beach, S. R. (n.d.). 5 mindfulness practices to bring to your classroom. *Left Brain Buddha*. Retrieved from https://leftbrainbuddha.com/5-mindfulness-practices -bring-classroom/

Bellinger, D. B., DeCaro, M. S., & Ralston, P. A. (2015). Mindfulness, anxiety, and high-stakes mathematics performance in the laboratory and classroom. *Consciousness and Cognition, 37*, 123–132.

Berkowicz, J., & Myers, A. (2014, August 24). Compassion in the classroom: A "real strength" for education. *Education Week*. Retrieved from http://blogs.edweek. org/edweek/leadership_360/2014/08/compassion_in_the_classroom_a_real_ strength_for_education.html

Berl, R. P. (2015, October 7). Schools are now teaching kids—and their parents—how to deal with stress. *Washington Post*. Retrieved from https://www.washingtonpost .com/lifestyle/on-parenting/teaching-kids—and-parents—the-art-of-mindfulness/2015/10/06/d0519c6a-65fd-11e5-9223-70cb36460919_story. html?utm_term=.c097a44af174

Biegel, G. M., Brown, K. W., Shapiro, S. L., & Schubert, C. M. (2009). Mindfulness-based stress reduction for the treatment of adolescent psychiatric outpatients: A randomized clinical trial. *Consulting and Clinical Psychology, 77*(5), 855–866.

Birkerts, S. (2006). *The Gutenberg elegies: The fate of reading in an electronic age*. New York: Farrar, Straus and Giroux.

Blad, E. (2017, November 21). Adults send children mixed messages about kindness: Here's why that matters to schools. *Education Week*. Retrieved from https:// blogs.edweek.org/edweek/rulesforengagement/2017/11/adults_send_children _mixed_messages_about_kindness_heres_why_that_matters_to_schools .html?r=298434214

Bloom, D. (2016, November 8). Instead of detention, these students get meditation. *CNN Health.* Retrieved from https://www.cnn.com/2016/11/04/health /meditation-in-schools-baltimore/index.html

Bluth, K., & Blanton, P. W. (2014). Mindfulness and self-compassion: Exploring pathways to adolescent emotional well-being. *Journal of Child and Family Studies, 23*(7), 1298–1309.

Bluth, K., Gaylord, S. A., Campo R. A., Mullarkey, M. C., & Hobbs, L. (2016). Making friends with yourself: A mixed methods pilot study of a mindful self-compassion program for adolescents. *Mindfulness, 7*(2), 479–492.

Boccella, K. (2018, February 9). After last year's brawl, Cheltenham schools try mindfulness to keep the peace. *Inquirer.* Retrieved from http://www2.philly .com/philly/education/brawl-cheltenham-schools-mindfulness-promote-good -behavior-20180209.html

Booth, R. (2017, October 13). "Way ahead of the curve": UK hosts first summit on mindful politics. *The Guardian.* Retrieved from https://www.theguardian.com /lifeandstyle/2017/oct/13/politicians-meditate-commons-mindfulness-event

Borsuk, A. (2015, November 28). West Milwaukee school finds a mindful minute goes a long way. *Milwaukee Wisconsin Journal-Sentinel.* Retrieved from http://archive .jsonline.com/news/education/west-milwaukee-school-finds-a-mindful-minute -goes-a-long-way-b99622574z1-357049241.html

Bowen, S., Witkiewitz, K., Clifasefi, S. L., Grow, J., Chawla, N., Hsu, S. H., et al. (2014). Relative efficacy of mindfulness-based relapse prevention, standard relapse prevention, and treatment as usual for substance use disorders: A randomized clinical trial. *JAMA Psychiatry, 71*(5): 547–556.

Boyce, B. (2015, November 26). NBA's winningest team guided by mindfulness and joy. *Mindful.* Retrieved from https://www.mindful.org/nbas-winningest-team -guided-by-mindfulness-and-joy/

Brackett, M. A. (2016, Summer). The emotion revolution. *Independent School.* Retrieved from https://www.nais.org/magazine/independent-school/ summer-2016/the-emotion-revolution/

Brady, R. (2005, Winter/Spring). Mindfulness & mathematics: Teaching as a deep learning process. *Mindfulness Bell.* Retrieved from https://www.mindfulnessbell .org/archive/2015/06/mindfulness-mathematics

Bream, R. (2018, March 8). Riverside intermediate teacher ties compassion into curriculum. *Fishers Patch.* Retrieved from https://patch.com/indiana/fishers /riverside-intermediate-teacher-ties-compassion-curriculum

Breines, J. G., Thoma, M. V., Gianferante, D., Hanlin, L., Chen, X., & Rohleder, N. (2014, March). Self-compassion as a predictor of interleukin-6 response to acute psychosocial stress. *Brain Behavior and Immunity, 37,* 109–114.

Britton, W. B., Lepp, N. E., Niles, H. F., Rocha, T., Fisher, N., & Gold, J. (2014). A randomized controlled pilot trial of classroom-based mindfulness meditation compared to an active control condition in 6th grade children. *Journal of School Psychology, 52*(3), 263–278.

Broderick, P. C., & Frank, J. L. (2014, Summer). Learning to BREATHE: An intervention to foster mindfulness in adolescence. *New Directions for Youth Development,* (142), 31–44.

Broderick, P. C., & Jennings, P. A. (2012, Winter). Mindfulness for adolescents: A promising approach to supporting emotion regulation and preventing risky behavior. *New Directions for Youth Development,* (136), 111–126.

Broncaccio, D. (2018, February 13). Taking a breath: What Colrain kids learn about "mindfulness." *Greenfield Recorder.* Retrieved from https://www.recorder.com /Taking-a-breath-What-Colrain-kids-learn-about-mindfulness-15501000

Brown, P. L. (2007, June 16). In the classroom, a new focus on quieting the mind. *New York Times.* Retrieved from https://www.nytimes.com/2007/06/16/us/16mindful .html

Buffum, J. (2017, January 11). Mindful classrooms: Teaching kids to cope, one breath at a time. *New Jersey Monthly.* Retrieved from https://njmonthly.com/articles /health/yoga-in-schools-mindful-classrooms/

Canty, E. (2017, September 1). When kindness is in the curriculum. *Good Education.* Retrieved from https://education.good.is/articles/kindness-in-the-curriculum

Carter, D. (2015, November 27). Kids use meditation, mindfulness to de-stress. *Courier-Journal.* Retrieved from https://www.courier-journal.com/story /life/wellness/fitness/2015/11/27/kids-use-meditation-mindfulness -de-stress/74240432/

CASEL. (2012). *Effective social and emotional learning programs.* Retrieved from https://casel.org/wp-content/uploads/2016/01/2013-casel-guide-1.pdf

Cassone, A. R. (2015). Mindfulness training as an adjunct to evidence-based treatment for ADHD within families. *Journal of Attention Disorders, 19*(2), 147–157.

CAST. (2018). Universal Design for Learning Guidelines version 2.2. Retrieved from http://udlguidelines.cast.org

CBS News. (2016, October 26). How meditation is making a "huge difference" in one Baltimore school. *CBS This Morning.* Retrieved from https://www.cbsnews.com /news/meditation-students-mindful-moments-program-robert-w-coleman -elementary-school/

Center for Healthy Minds. (2017, Summer). A mindfulness-based kindness curriculum for preschoolers. Retrieved from https://centerhealthyminds.org/join-the -movement/sign-up-to-receive-the-kindness-curriculum

Center on the Developing Child. (2018). Toxic stress. Harvard University. Retrieved from https://developingchild.harvard.edu/science/key-concepts/toxic-stress/

Chiesa, A., Serretti, A., & Jakobsen, J. (2013, February). Mindfulness: Top-down or bottom-up emotion regulation strategy? *Clinical Psychology Review, 33*(1), 82–96.

Cho, H., Ryu, S., Noh, J., & Lee, J. (2016). The effectiveness of daily mindful breathing practices on test anxiety of students. *PLOS ONE, 11*(10).

Clinton, V., Swenseth, M., & Carlson, S. E. (2018). Do mindful breathing exercises benefit reading comprehension? A brief report. *Journal of Cognitive Enhancement, 2*(3), 305–310.

Colias-Pete, M. (2018, January 20). Merrillville school hopes to see suspensions drop with new meditation offering. *Chicago Tribune.* Retrieved from https://www .chicagotribune.com/suburbs/post-tribune/news/ct-ptb-merrillville-miller -elementary-mindfulness-st-0122-20180121-story.html

Cone, S. (2016, November 16). No place like ommm: Schools are incorporating mindfulness as a way to help children develop better. *Sun*. Retrieved from http://www.santamariasun.com/cover/15381/no-place-like-ommm-schools-are-incorporating-mindfulness-as-a-way-to-help-children-develop-better/

Constantinescu, L. (2012, March 9). Art and mindfulness: Art can shock us into the present moment. *Mindfulword*. Retrieved from https://www.themindfulword.org/2012/art-mindfulness-present-moment/

Cook-Deegan, P. (2014, August 11). Eight tips for teaching mindfulness in high school. *Greater Good Magazine*. Retrieved from https://greatergood.berkeley.edu/article/item/eight_tips_for_teaching_mindfulness_in_high_school

Copeland, W., Shanahan, L., Costello, E. J., & Angold, A. (2011). Cumulative prevalence of psychiatric disorders by young adulthood: A prospective cohort analysis from the Great Smoky Mountains Study. *Journal of the American Academy of Child & Adolescent Psychiatry, 50*(3), 252–261.

Creswell, J. D. (2017). Mindfulness interventions. *Annual Review of Psychology, 68*, 491–516.

Creswell, J. D., & Lindsay, E. K. (2014). How does mindfulness training affect health? A mindfulness stress buffering account. *Current Directions in Psychological Science, 23*(6), 401–407.

Csikszentmihalyi, M. (2008). *Flow: The psychology of optimal experience*. New York: Harper Perennial.

Curtin, T. (2017, March 28). How a Waldorf teacher inspires mindfulness. Waldorf School of Cape Cod. Retrieved from https://www.waldorfschoolofcapecod.org/blog/how-a-waldorf-teacher-inspires-mindfulness

Curtis, M. (2016, January 15). Mindfulness meditation in a school library. *IFLA*. Retrieved from https://www.ifla.org/node/10132

Dalbey, B. (2018, April 6). Kindness challenge confronts bullying where it happens most. *Patch*. Retrieved from https://patch.com/us/across-america/kindness-challenge-confronts-bullying-where-it-happens-most

Daly, J. (2017, January 23). Mindfulness practices help students deal with stress, behavior. *Pittsburgh Post-Gazette*. Retrieved from http://www.post-gazette.com/news/health/2017/01/24/Mindfulness-practices-help-students-deal-with-stress-behavior/stories/201701170001

Davenport, M. (2018, February 1). Mindfulness in high school. *Edutopia*. Retrieved from https://www.edutopia.org/article/mindfulness-high-school

Davidson, R. J., Kabat-Zinn, J., Schumacher, J., Rosenkranz, M., Muller, D., Santorelli, S. F., et al. (2003, July-August). Alterations in brain and immune function produced by mindfulness meditation. *Psychosomatic Medicine, 65*(4), 564–570.

Davis, L. C. (2015, August 31). When mindfulness meets the classroom. *Atlantic*. Retrieved from https://www.theatlantic.com/education/archive/2015/08/mindfulness-education-schools-meditation/402469/

Deak, J., & Deak, T. (2013). *The owner's manual for driving your adolescent brain*. San Francisco: Little Pickle Press.

de Bruin, E. I., Blom, R., Smit, F. M. A., van Steensel, F. J. A., & Bögels, S. M. (2015) MYmind: Mindfulness training for youngsters with autism spectrum disorders and their parents. *Autism, 19*(8), 906–914.

DeRuy, E. (2016). Does mindfulness actually work in schools? *Atlantic*. Retrieved from https://www.theatlantic.com/education/archive/2016/05/testing-mindfulness-in-the-early-years/483749/

DeWitt, P. (2016, January 29). Mindful leaders are key for transforming school [blog post]. *Education Week*. Retrieved from http://blogs.edweek.org/edweek/finding_common_ground/2016/01/be_mindful_redefining_school_leadership_transforming_you_and_your_school.html?r=225959388

Ditto, B., Eclache, M., & Goldman, N. (2006). Short-term autonomic and cardiovascular effects of mindfulness body scan meditation. *Annals of Behavioral Medicine, 32*(3), 227–234.

Dorman, E. (2015). Building teachers' social-emotional competence through mindfulness practices. *Curriculum and Teaching Dialogue, 17*(1–2), 103–119.

Dunn School. (2018). Math meets mindfulness at middle school. Retrieved from https://www.dunnschool.org/math-meets-mindfulness-at-the-middle-school

Durlak, J. A., Weissberg, R. P., Dymnicki, A. B., Taylor, R. D., & Schellinger, K. B. (2011). The impact of enhancing students' social and emotional learning: A meta-analysis of school-based universal interventions. *Child Development, 82*(1), 405–432.

Edwards, B. (2012). *Drawing on the right side of the brain* (4th ed.). New York: Tarcher/Penguin.

Eigsti, I. M., Zayas, V., Mischel, W., Shoda, Y., Ayduk, O., Dadlani, M. B., et al. (2006). Predicting cognitive control from preschool to late adolescence and young adulthood. *Psychological Science, 17*(6), 478–484.

Emerson, L-M., Leyland, A., Hudson, K., Rowse, G., Hanley, P., & Hugh-Jones, S. (2017). Teaching mindfulness to teachers: A systematic review and narrative synthesis. *Mindfulness, 8*(5), 1136–1149.

Engel, S., & Sandstrom, M. (2010, July 22). There's only one way to stop a bully. *New York Times*. Retrieved from https://www.nytimes.com/2010/07/23/opinion/23engel.html

Flook, L., Goldberg, S. B., Pinger, L., Bonus, K., & Davidson, R. J. (2013). Mindfulness for teachers: A pilot study to assess effects on stress, burnout and teaching efficacy. *Mind, Brain, and Education, 7*(3). Retrieved from https://www.ncbi.nlm.nih.gov/pmc/articles/PMC3855679/

Flook, L., Goldberg, S. B., Pinger, L., & Davidson, R. J. (2015). Promoting prosocial behavior and self-regulatory skills in preschool children through a mindfulness-based kindness curriculum. *Developmental Psychology, 51*(1), 44–51.

Flook, L., & Pinger, L. (n.d.). Lessons from creating a kindness curriculum. Center for Healthy Minds, University of Wisconsin–Madison. Retrieved from https://centerhealthyminds.org/join-the-movement/lessons-from-creating-a-kindness-curriculum

Flook, L., Smalley, S. L., Kitil, M. J., Galla, B. M., Kaiser-Greenland, S., Locke, J., et al. (2010). Effects of mindfulness awareness practices on executive functions in elementary school children. *Journal of Applied School Psychology, 26*(1), 70–95.

Forbes, D. (2015, November 8). They want kids to be robots: Meet the new education craze designed to distract you from overtesting. *Slate*. Retrieved from https://www.salon.com/2015/11/08/they_want_kids_to_be_robots_meet_the_new_education_craze_designed_to_distract_you_from_overtesting/

Gallup. (2014). *State of America's schools report: The path to winning again in education.* Retrieved from https://www.gallup.com/services/178769/state-america-schools-report.aspx

Garland, E. L., Baker, A. K., Larsen, P., Riquino, M. R., Priddy, S. E., Thomas, E., et al. (2017). Randomized controlled trial of brief mindfulness training and hypnotic suggestion for acute pain relief in the hospital setting. *Journal of General Internal Medicine, 32*(10), 1106–1113.

Garrison Institute. (2009, April 10). Garrison Institute's CARE program for teachers receives federal funding. Retrieved from https://www.garrisoninstitute.org/wp-content/uploads/2015/10/Garrison_Institute_IES_grant_10Apr09.pdf

Gelles, D. (2017, July 19). How to be mindful while reading. *New York Times.* Retrieved from https://www.nytimes.com/2017/07/19/well/mind/how-to-be-mindful-while-reading.html

Gerszberg, C. O. (2018). Mindfulness in education. *Mindful.* Retrieved from https://www.mindful.org/mindfulness-in-education/

Giles, W., Hunt, H., Lewallen, T. C., Potts-Datema, W., & Slade, S. (2014). *Whole school, whole community, whole child: A collaborative approach to learning and health.* CDC/ASCD. Retrieved from http://www.ascd.org/ASCD/pdf/siteASCD/publications/wholechild/wscc-a-collaborative-approach.pdf

Girod, M., Twyman, T., & Wojcikiewicz, S. (2010). Teaching and learning science for transformative, aesthetic experience. *Journal of Science Teacher Education, 21*(7), 801–824.

Glazer, E. (2011, March 28). Namaste. Now nap time. *Wall Street Journal.* Retrieved from https://www.wsj.com/articles/SB10001424052748703386704576186463216602684

Gomstyn, A. (2018). A class act: How mindfulness is helping to transform schools. *Aetna.* Retrieved from https://www.aetna.com/health-guide/mindfulness-transform-schools.html

Gonzalez, L. (2018, February). Becoming a more mindful school leader. *District Administrator.* Retrieved from https://www.districtadministration.com/article/becoming-more-mindful-school-leader

Greenwich Free Press. (2017, September 25). Combating stress: Greenwich students exercise mindfulness in the moment. Retrieved from https://greenwichfreepress.com/schools/combating-stress-greenwich-students-exercise-mindfulness-in-the-moment-95128/

Gu, Y., Xu, G., & Zhu, Y. (2018). A randomized controlled trial of mindfulness-based cognitive therapy for college students with ADHD. *Journal of Attention Disorders, 22*(4), 388–399.

Hall, M. P., O'Hare, A., Santavicca, N., & Jones, L. F. (2015). The power of deep reading and mindful literacy: An innovative approach in contemporary education. *Innovación Educativa, 15*(67), 49–59.

Hallabeck, E. (2018, June 22). Reed sixth graders run "kindness carts." *Newtown Bee.* Retrieved from https://www.newtownbee.com/reed-sixth-graders-run-kindness-carts

Hattie, J. (2008). *Visible learning: A synthesis of over 800 meta-analyses relating to achievement.* London: Routledge.

Heckman, J. J. (2008, May). *Schools, skills, and synapses*. Working Paper No. 3515. Bonn, Germany: Institute for the Study of Labor. Retrieved from https://heckmanequation.org/assets/2017/01/Schools_Skills_Synapsis.pdf

Heckman, J. J. (2011). The economics of inequality: The value of early childhood education. *American Educator, 35*(1), 31–35.

Heckman, J. J., Moon, S. H., Pinto, R., Savelyev, P. A., & Yavitz, A. (2010). The rate of return to the High/Scope Perry Preschool Program. *Journal of Public Economics, 94*(1–2), 114–128.

Herman, K. C., Hickmon-Rosa, J., & Reinke, W. M. (2017). Empirically derived profiles of teacher stress, burnout, self-efficacy, and coping and associated student outcomes. *Journal of Positive Behavior Interventions, 20*(2), 90–100.

Hölzel, B. K., Carmody, J., Evans, K. C., Hoge, E. A., Dusek, J. A., & Morgan, L., (2010). Stress reduction correlates with structural changes in the amygdala. *Social, Cognitive, and Affective Neuroscience, 5*(1), 11–17.

Hölzel, B. K., Carmody, J., Vangel, M., Congleton, C., Yerramsetti, S. M., Gard, T., et al. (2011). Mindfulness practice leads to increases in regional brain gray matter density. *Psychiatry Research, 191*(1), 36–43.

Hsu, F. (2016). What is the sound of one invisible hand clapping? Neoliberalism, the invisibility of Asian and Asian American Buddhists, and secular mindfulness in education. In R. E. Purser, D. Forbes, & A. Burke (Eds.), *Handbook of mindfulness: Culture, context, and social engagement* (pp. 369–381). New York: Springer.

Jennings, P. A., Brown, J. L., Frank, J. L., Doyle, S., Oh, Y., Davis, R., et al. (2017). Impacts of the CARE for Teachers program on teachers' social and emotional competence and classroom interactions. *Journal of Educational Psychology, 109*(7), 1010–1028.

Jennings, P. A., Frank, J. L., Snowberg, K. E., Coccia, M. A., & Greenberg, M. T. (2013). Improving classroom learning environments by Cultivating Awareness and Resilience in Education (CARE): Results of a randomized controlled trial. *School Psychology Quarterly, 28*(4), 374–390.

Johnson, C., Burke, C., Brinkman, S., & Wade, T. (2016). Effectiveness of a school-based mindfulness program for transdiagnostic prevention in young adolescents. *Behavior Research and Therapy, 81*, 1–11.

Jones, D. E., Greenberg, M., & Crowley, M. (2015). Early social-emotional functioning and public health: The relationship between kindergarten social competence and future wellness. *American Journal of Public Health, 105*(11), 2283–2290.

Jupin, A. (2016, September 26). Mindfulness helps children as young as 3 manage their emotions during school. *UCLA Newsroom*. Retrieved from http://newsroom.ucla.edu/stories/mindfulness-helps-children-as-young-as-3-manage-their-emotions-during-school

Kabat-Zinn, J. (2005). *Wherever you go, there you are: Mindfulness meditation in everyday life*. New York: Hachette.

Kabat-Zinn, J. (2013). *Full catastrophe living: Using the wisdom of your body and mind to face stress, pain, and illness* (Rev. ed.). New York: Bantam Books.

Kaleem, J. (2017, December 6). Reading, writing, required silence: How meditation is changing schools and students. *Huffington Post*. Retrieved from https://www.huffingtonpost.com/2015/06/12/schools-meditation-quiet-time_n_7544582.html?guccounter=1

Kamenetz, A. (2016, August 19). When teachers take a breath, students can bloom. NPR. Retrieved from https://www.npr.org/sections/ed/2016/08/19/488866975/when-teachers-take-a-breath-students-can-bloom

Katterman, S. N., Kleinman, B. M., Hood, M. M., Nackers, L. M., & Corsica, J. A. (2014). Mindfulness meditation as an intervention for binge eating, emotional eating, and weight loss: A systematic review. *Eating Behaviors, 15*(2), 197–204.

Kelly, C. (2016, June 7). Beware "McMindfulness": If you're going to embed mindfulness in your school, do it properly. *Teachwire.* Retrieved from https://www.teachwire.net/news/beware-mcmindfulness-if-youre-going-to-embed-mindfulness-in-your-school-do

Kerr, S., O'Donovan, A., & Pepping, C. (2015, March). Can gratitude and kindness interventions enhance wellbeing in a clinical sample? *Journal of Happiness Studies, 16*(1), 17–36.

Killingsworth, M. A., & Gilbert, D. T. (2010). A wandering mind is an unhappy mind. *Science, 330*(6006), 932.

Kilpatrick, L. A., Suyenobu, B. Y., Smith, S. R., Bueller, J. A., Goodman, T., Creswell, J. D., et al. (2011). Impact of Mindfulness-Based Stress Reduction training on intrinsic brain connectivity. *Neuroimage, 56*(1), 290–298.

Kim, J., & Kwon, M. (2018, January). Effects of mindfulness-based intervention to improve task performance for children with intellectual disabilities. *Journal of Applied Research in Intellectual Disabilities, 31*(1), 87–97.

King, J. (2017, December 26). Here's how mindfulness helps schools address depression and anxiety. *Deseret News.* Retrieved from https://www.deseretnews.com/article/900006177/heres-how-mindfulness-helps-schools-address-depression-and-anxiety.html

Klingbeil, D., Renshaw, T., Willenbrink, J., Copek, R., Chan, K., & Haddock, A. (2017, August). Mindfulness-based interventions with youth: A comprehensive meta-analysis of group-design studies. *Journal of School Psychology, 63,* 77–103.

Kolb, B., & Gibb, R. (2011, November). Brain plasticity and behaviour in the developing brain. *Journal of the Canadian Academy of Child and Adolescent Psychiatry, 20*(4), 265-276.

Kuyken, W., Byford, S., Taylor, R. S., Watkins, E., Holden, E., White, K., et al. (2008). Mindfulness-based cognitive therapy to prevent relapse in recurrent depression. *Journal of Consulting and Clinical Psychology, 76*(6), 966–978.

Landau, M. D. (2018, February 2). Why you should urge your child's teacher to have classroom yoga breaks. *Huffington Post.* Retrieved from https://www.huffingtonpost.com/meryl-davids-landau/why-you-should-urge-your-_b_14550058.html

Langer, E. (2014). *Mindfulness* (25th anniversary ed.) Cambridge, MA: Da Capo Press.

Lantieri, L., & Zakrzewski, V. (2015, April 7). How SEL and mindfulness can work together. *Greater Good Magazine.* Retrieved from https://greatergood.berkeley.edu/article/item/how_social_emotional_learning_and_mindfulness_can_work_together

Layous, K., Nelson, S. K., Oberle, E., Schonert-Reichl, K. A., & Lyubomirsky, S. (2012). Kindness counts: Prompting prosocial behavior in preadolescents boosts peer acceptance and well-being. *PLOS ONE, 7*(12). Retrieved from https://www.ncbi.nlm.nih.gov/pmc/articles/PMC3530573/

Lazar, S. W., Kerr, C. E., Wasserman, R. H., Gray, J. R., Greve, D. N., Treadway, M. T., et al. (2005). Meditation experience is associated with increased cortical thickness. *Neuroreport, 16*(17), 1893–1897.

Lemberger-Truelove, M. E., Carbonneau, K. J., Atencio, D. J., Zieher, A. K., & Palacios, A. F. (2018). Self-regulatory growth effects for young children participating in a combined social and emotional learning and mindfulness-based intervention. *Journal of Counseling & Development, 96*(3), 289–302.

Lenhart, A., Madden, M., Smith, A., Purcell, K., & Zickuhr, K. (2011, November 9). Teens, kindness and cruelty on social network sites. Pew Research Center. Retrieved from http://www.pewinternet.org/2011/11/09/teens-kindness-and -cruelty-on-social-network-sites/

Levin, M. (2017, June 12). Why Google, Nike, and Apple love mindfulness training, and how you can easily love it too. *Inc.* Retrieved from https://www.inc.com/marissa -levin/why-google-nike-and-apple-love-mindfulness-training-and-how-you-can -easily-love-.html

Lin, J. W., & Mai, L. J. (2018). Impact of mindfulness meditation intervention on academic performance. *Innovations in Education and Teaching International, 55*(3), 366–375.

Linan, A. (2018, April 3). Mindfulness program offered in Las Cruces decreases stress. *Las Cruces Sun-News.* Retrieved from https://www.lcsun-news.com/story /life/wellness/2018/04/03/mindfulness-program-las-cruses-decrease-stress -health/429594002/

Luders, E., Toga, A. W., Lepore, N., & Gaser, C. (2009). The underlying anatomical correlates of long-term meditation: Larger hippocampal and frontal volumes of gray matter. *Neuroimage, 45*(3), 672–678.

Lueke, A., & Gibson, B. (2014). Mindfulness meditation reduces implicit age and race bias: The role of reduced automaticity of responding. *Social Psychological and Personality Science, 6*(3), 284–291.

Lunau, K. (2014, June 15). Bringing mindfulness to the school curriculum. *Maclean's.* Retrieved from https://www.macleans.ca/society/health/bringing-mindfulness -to-the-school-curriculum/

Machado, A. (2014, January 27). Should schools teach kids to meditate? *Atlantic.* Retrieved from https://www.theatlantic.com/education/archive/2014/01/should -schools-teach-kids-to-meditate/283229/

Marsh, I. C., Chan, S. W. Y., & MacBeth, A. (2018, August). Self-compassion and psychological distress in adolescents—a meta-analysis. *Mindfulness, 9*(4), 1011–1027.

Marshall, A. (2017, November 21). Can mindfulness improve school performance? *Louisville Magazine.* Retrieved from https://www.louisville.com/content /compassionate-curriculum

Marshall, S. L., Parker, P. D., Ciarrochi, J., Sahdra, B., Jackson, C. J., & Heaven, P. C. L. (2015). Self-compassion protects against the negative effects of low self-esteem: A longitudinal study in a large adolescent sample. *Personality and Individual Differences, 74,* 116–121.

Maynard, B. R., Solis, M. R., Miller, V. L., & Brendel, K. E. (2017, March 10). Mindfulness-based interventions for improving cognition, academic achievement, behavior, and socioemotional functioning of primary and secondary school students. Retrieved from https://campbellcollaboration.org/media/k2/attachments/Campbell_systematic_review_-_Mindfulness_and_school_students.pdf

McLean, L., Abry, T., Taylor, M., & Connor, C. M. (2018, August). Associations among teachers' depressive symptoms and students' classroom instructional experiences in third grade. *Journal of School Psychology, 69*, 154–168.

Mead, R. (2017, December 11). Success Academy's radical educational experiment. *The New Yorker*. Retrieved from https://www.newyorker.com/magazine/2017/12/11/success-academys-radical-educational-experiment

Miller, K. (2012, August 28). Teaching compassion: Changing the world through empathy and education. *ParentMap*. Retrieved from https://www.parentmap.com/article/compassion-changing-the-world-through-empathy-and-education

Mindfulschools.org. (2018). Why mindfulness is needed in education. Retrieved from https://www.mindfulschools.org/about-mindfulness/mindfulness-in-education/

Mischel, W. (2015). *The marshmallow test: Why self-control is the engine of success*. New York: Back Bay Books.

Moffitt, T. E., Arseneault, L., Belsky, D., Dickson, N., Hancox, R. J., Harrington, H., et al. (2011). A gradient of childhood self-control predicts health, wealth, and public safety. *Proceedings of the National Academy of Sciences, 108*(7), 2693–2698.

Monfredo, J. (2018, May 6). Monfredo: The buddy bench—A symbol of kindness in our schools. *Worcester.com*. Retrieved from http://www.golocalworcester.com/news/monfredo-the-buddy-bench-a-symbol-of-kindness-in-our-schools

Monto, M. A., McRee, N., & Deryck, F. S. (2018, August). Nonsuicidal self-injury among a representative sample of U.S. adolescents, 2015. *American Journal of Public Health, 108*(8), 1042–1048.

Mrazek, M. D., Franklin, M. S., Phillips, D. T., Baird, B., & Schooler, J. W. (2013). Mindfulness training improves working memory capacity and GRE performance while reducing mind wandering. *Psychological Science, 24*(5), 776–781.

Mundasad, S. (2015, July 15). Mindfulness classes to "help teenagers' mental fitness." *BBC News*. Retrieved from https://www.bbc.com/news/health-33540242

Myers, M. (2015, June 1). Improving military resilience through mindfulness training. *USAMRMC Public Affairs*. Retrieved from https://www.army.mil/article/149615/improving_military_resilience_through_mindfulness_training

National Health Service. (2016, June 1). Five steps to mental wellbeing. Retrieved from https://www.nhs.uk/conditions/stress-anxiety-depression/improve-mental-wellbeing/

NBA Communications. (2018, March 20). NBA teams up with leading mindfulness app Headspace to provide training and resources to league and team staff. Retrieved from http://pr.nba.com/nba-teams-up-with-headspace/

New Harbinger Publications. (2015, February 5). Study finds ethnically diverse, at-risk adolescents highly receptive to mindfulness classes. Retrieved from https://www.newharbinger.com/blog/study-finds-ethnically-diverse-risk-adolescents-highly-receptive-mindfulness-classes

Oberle, E., & Schonert-Reichl, K. A. (2016, June). Stress contagion in the classroom? The link between classroom teacher burnout and morning cortisol in elementary school students. *Social Science & Medicine, 159,* 30–37.

Palta, P., Page, G., Piferi, R. L., Gill, J. M., Hayat, M. J., Connolly, A. B., et al. (2012). Evaluation of a mindfulness-based intervention program to decrease blood pressure in low-income African-American older adults. *Journal of Urban Health, 89*(2), 308–316.

Parker, S. (2018, April 28). Christians object to this school's yoga "mindfulness" routine. *KING5.* Retrieved from https://www.king5.com/article/news/nation -now/christians-object-to-this-schools-yoga-mindfulness-routine/465-afd7c44d -54fd-4bc9-8982-ad61d9c5502e

PBS NewsHour. (2017, February 21). Faced with outsized stresses, these Baltimore students learn to take a deep breath [transcript]. Retrieved from https://www .pbs.org/newshour/show/faced-outsized-stresses-baltimore-students-learn -take-deep-breath

Perry, T. (2015, June 12). Legal fight against yoga in Encinitas schools is finished. *Los Angeles Times.* Retrieved from http://www.latimes.com/local/lanow/la-me-ln -yoga-legal-fight-20150612-story.html#

Philpott, A. (2018, March 1). Central Kentucky schools turning to yoga to combat stress. *WKYT.* Retrieved from https://www.wkyt.com/content/news/Central -Kentucky-schools-turning-to-yoga-to-combat-stress-475593193.html

Piaget, J., & Inhelder, B. (2013). *The growth of logical thinking from childhood to adolescence: An essay on the construction of formal operational structures.* New York: Routledge.

Pinger, L., & Flook, L. (2016, February 1). What if schools taught kindness? *Greater Good Magazine.* Retrieved from https://greatergood.berkeley.edu/article/item /what_if_schools_taught_kindness

Pinsker, G. (2015, March 30). Mindfulness program at John Adams Middle School enhances school climate [press release]. Santa Monica–Malibu Unified School District. Retrieved from http://www.smmusd.org/press/press1415 /MindfulnessAtJAMS.pdf

Plantier, R. (2017, December 6). This Washington DC public elementary school teaches mindfulness every week. *Huffington Post.* Retrieved from https://www .huffingtonpost.com/rebeca-plantier/this-washington-dc-public_b_8207536 .html

Playfield Institute (n.d.). Mindfulness. Retrieved from https://www.handsonscotland .co.uk/mindfulness/

Possemato, K., Bergen-Cico, D., Treatman, S., Allen, C., Wade, M., & Pigeon, W. (2016). A randomized clinical trial of primary care brief mindfulness training for veterans with PTSD. *Journal of Clinical Psychology, 72*(3), 179–193.

Quach, D., Jastrowski Mano, K. E., & Alexander, K. (2016). A randomized controlled trial examining the effect of mindfulness meditation on working memory capacity in adolescents, *Journal of Adolescent Health, 58*(5), 489–496.

Quintiliani, A. (2015, June 7). Mindfulness organizational and school climate: The variables. *Mindful Happiness.* Retrieved from http://mindfulhappiness.org/2015 /mindfulness-organizational-and-school-climate-the-variables/

Rascon, D. (2017, December 6). Valley High School students learn to cope with stress in "mindfulness room." *2KUTV*. Retrieved from https://kutv.com/news/local /meditation-yoga-drumming-the-future-of-education

Ratnala, S. (2018, January 30). When physics meets yoga. *Medium*. Retrieved from https://medium.com/@sujatha.ratnala/when-physics-meets-yoga -4251c00639cd

Redford, K. (2018, May 30). What happened when I committed to loving my students unconditionally. *Education Week Teacher*. Retrieved from https://www.edweek .org/tm/articles/2018/05/30/what-happens-when-i-love-my-students -unconditionally.html

Regents of the University of California. (2014). Relevant research. Retrieved from https://sites.uci.edu/mindfulhs/relevant-research/

Resnick, B. (2017, October 19). Is mindfulness meditation good for kids? Here's what the science actually says. *Vox*. Retrieved from https://www.vox.com/science-and -health/2017/5/22/13768406/mindfulness-meditation-good-for-kids-evidence

Reynolds, E. (2018, January). Mindfulness—The potential for calmer, clearer-minded and more content teachers and pupils. *APAC ELT Journal*. Retrieved from https://agora.xtec.cat/iesjoanot/wp-content/uploads/usu589/2018/02 /January_2018-Issue_86.pdf

Roeser, R. W., Schonert-Reichl, K. A., Jha, A., Cullen, M., Wallace, L., Wilensky, R., et al. (2013, April 29). Mindfulness training and reductions in teacher stress and burnout: Results from two randomized, waitlist-control field trials. *Journal of Educational Psychology, 105*(3), 787–804.

Room 241 Team. (2018, February 14). Mindfulness activities for the elementary classroom. Room 241. Retrieved from https://education.cu-portland.edu/blog /classroom-resources/mindfulness-activities-kids-classroom/

Rose, D., & Meyer, A. (2002). *Teaching every student in the digital age: Universal design for learning*. Alexandria, VA: ASCD.

Ruiz, R. (2018, April 29). The skills that every teen should learn before they ever get a cellphone. *Mashable*. Retrieved from https://mashable.com/2018/04/29 /teenage-cell-phone-addiction-mental-health-mindfulness/#whldCK.c4iqa

Ryan, T. (2012). *A mindful nation: How a simple practice can help us reduce stress, improve performance, and recapture the American spirit*. Carlsbad, CA: Hay House.

Ryden, L. (2018, March 9). My students call me the "peace teacher." My job has never felt more important. *Washington Post*. Retrieved from https://www .washingtonpost.com/news/inspired-life/wp/2018/03/09/my-students -call-me-the-peace-teacher-my-job-has-never-felt-more-important/?utm _term=.76110652d7e1

Salmoirago-Blotcher, E., Druker, S., Frisard, C., Dunsiger, S. I. , Crawford, S., Meleo- Meyer, F., et al. (2018, January 28). Integrating mindfulness training in school health education to promote healthy behaviors in adolescents: Feasibility and preliminary effects on exercise and dietary habits. *Preventive Medicine Reports, 9*, 92–95.

Saltzman, A., & Goldin, P. (2008). Mindfulness-based stress reduction for school-aged children. In L. A. Greco and S. C. Hayes (Eds.). *Acceptance and mindfulness treatments for children and adolescents: A practitioner's guide* (pp. 139–161). Oakland, CA: New Harbinger Publications.

Sanger, K. L., & Dorjee, D. (2016). Mindfulness training with adolescents enhances metacognition and the inhibition of irrelevant stimuli: Evidence from event-related brain potentials. *Trends in Neuroscience and Education, 5*(1), 1–11.

Santas, D. (2016, May 10). Beyond "Namaste": The benefits of yoga in schools. *CNN Health.* Retrieved from https://www.cnn.com/2016/05/10/health/yoga-in -schools/index.html

Schachter, R. (2011, Winter). Can kindness be taught? *Scholastic.* Retrieved from https://www.scholastic.com/teachers/articles/teaching-content/can-kindness -be-taught/

Schimke, A. (2016, December 14). How Colorado schools are helping kids calm down— and learn—through mindfulness. *Chalkbeat.* Retrieved from https://chalkbeat. org/posts/co/2016/12/14/how-colorado-schools-are-helping-kids-calm-down -and-learn-through-mindfulness/

Scholastic. (n.d.). Lesson 4: Mindful listening. *The MindUP Curriculum, Grades Pre-K–2. Brain-Focused Strategies for Learning—and Living.* Retrieved from http:// teacher.scholastic.com/products/mindup/pdfs/Mindup_Prek-2_lesson.pdf

Schonert-Reichl, K. A., & Lawlor, M. S. (2010, September). The effects of a mindfulness-based education program on pre- and early adolescents' well-being and emotional and social competence. *Mindfulness, 1*(3), 137–151.

Schonert-Reichl, K. A., Oberle, E., Lawlor, M. S., Abbott, D., Thomson, K., Oberlander, T. F., et al. (2015, January). Enhancing cognitive and social-emotional development through a simple-to-administer mindfulness-based school program for elementary school children: A randomized controlled trial. *Developmental Psychology, 51*(1), 52–66.

Semple, R. J., Droutman, V., & Reid, B. A. (2017, January). Mindfulness goes to school: Things learned (so far) from research and real-world experiences. *Psychology in the Schools, 54*(1), 29–52.

Semple, R. J., & Lee, J. (2014). Mindfulness-based cognitive therapy for children. In R. Baer (Ed.), *Mindfulness-based treatment approaches: Clinician's guide to evidence base and applications* (pp. 161–188). Cambridge, MA: Academic Press.

Sesame Street in Communities. (n.d.). *Breathe* [video]. Retrieved from https:// sesamestreetincommunities.org/activities/breathe-bundle/

Shahidi, S., Akbari, H., & Zargar, F. (2017). Effectiveness of mindfulness-based stress reduction on emotion regulation and test anxiety in female high school students. *Journal of Education and Health Promotion, 6*, 87.

Shapiro, S. L., Lyons, K. E., Miller, R. C., Butler, B., Vieten, C., & Zelazo, P. D. (2015). Contemplation in the classroom: A new direction for improving childhood education. *Educational Psychology Review, 27*(1), 1–30.

Sharp, J. E., & Jennings, P. A. (2015). Strengthening teacher presence through mindfulness: What educators say about the Cultivating Awareness and Resilience in Education (CARE) program. *Mindfulness, 7*(1), 209–218.

Sibinga, E. M., Webb, L., Ghazarian, S. R., & Ellen, J. M. (2016). School-based mindfulness instruction: An RCT. *Pediatrics, 137*(1).

Siegel, D. J. (2015). *Brainstorm: The power and purpose of the teenage brain.* New York: Tarcher/Penguin.

Simmons, R. (2018, February 20). The promise of self-compassion for stressed-out teens. *New York Times*. Retrieved from https://www.nytimes.com/2018/02/20/well/family/self-compassion-stressed-out-teens.html

Sparks, S. D. (2017, July 3). Pre-test jitters? Here's how teachers are helping students de-stress. *PBS NewsHour*. Retrieved from https://www.pbs.org/newshour/education/pre-test-jitters-heres-teachers-helping-students-de-stress

Sparks, S. D., & Klein, A. (2018, April 24). Discipline disparities grow for students of color, new federal data show. *Education Week*. Retrieved from https://www.edweek.org/ew/articles/2018/04/24/discipline-disparities-grow-for-students-of-color.html?r=535968243

Spoon, M. (2017, January 19). Sesame Street brings UW center's kindness curriculum to kids. *University of Wisconsin–Madison News*. Retrieved from https://news.wisc.edu/sesame-street-brings-uw-centers-kindness-curriculum-to-kids/

Staats, C. (2015–2016). Understanding implicit bias: What educators should know. *American Educator*. Retrieved from https://www.aft.org/sites/default/files/ae_winter2015staats.pdf

Stevens, A. P. (2016, March 29). "Mindfulness" defuses stress in classrooms and teaching. *Science News for Students*. Retrieved from https://www.sciencenewsforstudents.org/article/%E2%80%98mindfulness%E2%80%99-defuses-stress-classrooms-and-teaching

Stopbullying.gov. (2017). Facts about bullying. Retrieved from https://www.stopbullying.gov/media/facts/index.html#stats

Strauss, E. (2016, March 2). Being mindful about mindfulness. *Slate*. Retrieved from http://www.slate.com/articles/double_x/family/2016/03/teaching_mindfulness_meditation_in_schools_a_skeptic_s_investigation.html

Sullivan, K. (2018, February 20). An education in kindness. *Monroe Monitor*. Retrieved from https://monroemonitor.com/Content/Default/Community/Article/An-education-in-kindness/-3/559/11055

Sung, K. (2018, June 18). Learning mindfulness centered on kindness to oneself and others. *KQED Mind Shift*. Retrieved from https://www.kqed.org/mindshift/51308/learning-mindfulness-centered-on-kindness-to-oneself-and-others

Taren, A. A., Gianaros, P. J., Greco, C. M., Lindsay, E. K., Fairgrieve, A., Brown, K. W., et al. (2015). Mindfulness meditation training alters stress-related amygdala resting state functional connectivity: A randomized controlled trial. *Social, Cognitive, and Affective Neuroscience, 10*(12), 1758–1768.

Tarrasch, R., Berman, Z., & Friedmann, N. (2016, May 10). Mindful reading: Mindfulness helps keep readers with dyslexia and ADHD on the lexical track. *Frontiers of Psychology, 7*, 578.

Taylor, C., Harrison, J. L., Haimovitz, K., Oberle, E., Thomson, K. C., Schonert-Reichl, K. A., et al. (2015). Examining ways that a mindfulness-based intervention reduces stress in public school teachers: A mixed-methods study. *Mindfulness, 7*(1).

Taylor, K. (2016, February 12). At Success Academy school, a stumble in math and a teacher's anger on video. *New York Times*. Retrieved from https://www.nytimes.com/2016/02/13/nyregion/success-academy-teacher-rips-up-student-paper.html

Taylor, V. A., Daneault, V., Grant, J., Scavone, G., Breton, E., Roffe-Vidal, S., et al. (2013). Impact of meditation training on the default mode network during a restful state. *Social, Cognitive, and Affective Neuroscience, 8*(1), 4–14.

Taylor, V. A., Grant, J., Daneault, V., Scavone, G., Breton, E., Roffe-Vidal, S., et al. (2011). Impact of mindfulness on the neural responses to emotional pictures in experienced and beginner meditators. *Neuroimage, 57*(4), 1524–1533.

Thomas, L. (2008). Being present: Mindfulness and yoga at Westminster Center School. *Horace, 24*(2). Retrieved from https://files.eric.ed.gov/fulltext/EJ849824.pdf

Unsworth, N., McMillan, B. D., Brewer, G. A., & Spillers, G. J. (2012). Everyday attention failures: An individual differences investigation. *Journal of Experimental Psychology, 38*(6), 1765–1772.

U.S. Department of Education. (2014). *Guiding principles: A resource guide for improving school climate and discipline.* Washington, DC: Author. Retrieved from https://www2.ed.gov/policy/gen/guid/school-discipline/guiding-principles.pdf

Viglas, M., & Perlman, M. (2018). Effects of a mindfulness-based program on young children's self-regulation, prosocial behavior, and hyperactivity. *Journal of Child and Family Studies, 27*(4), 1150–1161.

Volanen, S. M., Hankonen, N., Knittle, K., Beattie, M., Salo, G., & Suominen, S. (2015). Building resilience among adolescents: First results of a school-based mindfulness intervention: Salla-Maarit Volanen. *European Journal of Public Health, 25*(3).

Vøllestad, J., Sivertsen, B., & Nielsen, G. H. (2011). Mindfulness-based stress reduction for patients with anxiety disorders: Evaluation in a randomized controlled trial. *Behaviour Research and Therapy, 49*(4), 281–288.

Wagner, S. (2018, February 27). Compassion curriculum comes to life in JCPS. *WHAS11-ABC.* Retrieved from https://www.whas11.com/article/news/local/compassion-curriculum-comes-to-life-in-jcps/417-523471852

Ward, M. (2018, May 18). Do meditation apps work? *Sydney Morning Herald.* Retrieved from https://www.smh.com.au/lifestyle/health-and-wellness/do-meditation-apps-work-20180515-p4zfe8.html

Warsmith, S. (2013, April 14). Plain Township school stops "mindfulness" program after some in community raise concerns. *Beacon Journal.* Retrieved from https://www.ohio.com/akron/news/top-stories-news/plain-township-school-stops-mindfulness-program-after-some-in-community-raise-concern

Wells, C. M. (2015). Conceptualizing mindful leadership in schools: How the practice of mindfulness informs the practice of leading. *NCPEA Education Leadership Review of Doctoral Research, 2*(1), 1–23.

Whalen, D. J., Dixon-Gordon, K., Belden, A. C., Barch, D., & Luby, J. L. (2015). Correlates and consequences of suicidal cognitions and behaviors in children ages 3 to 7 years. *Journal of the American Academy of Child & Adolescent Psychiatry, 54*(11), 926–937.

Whitaker, R. C., Dearth-Wesley, T., & Gooze, R. A. (2015). Workplace stress and the quality of teacher–children relationships in Head Start. *Early Childhood Research Quarterly, 30*(A), 57–69.

Wieczner, C. (2016, March 12). Meditation has become a billion-dollar business. *Fortune.* Retrieved from http://fortune.com/2016/03/12/meditation-mindfulness-apps/

Will, M. (2017, June 7). Happy teachers practice self-care. *Education Week Teacher.* Retrieved from https://www.edweek.org/tm/articles/2017/06/07/social -emotional-competence-starts-at-the-head-of.html

Willard, C., & Nance, A. J. (2018, May 25). A mindful kids practice: The breath ball. *Mindful.* Retrieved from https://www.mindful.org/a-mindful-kids-practice-the -breath-ball/

Wilson, C. (2018, January 25). Mindful teachers make mindful students at Farragut Middle School. *lohud.* Retrieved from https://www.lohud.com/story/news /education/2018/01/16/farragut-middle-school-mindfulness/1017514001/

Wilson, E. O. (2000). *Sociobiology: The new synthesis* (25th anniversary ed.). Cambridge, MA: Belknap Press.

Wisner, B. L. (2014). An exploratory study of mindfulness meditation for alternative school students: Perceived benefits for improving school climate and student functioning. *Mindfulness, 5*(6), 626–638.

Yogi, M. M. (2001). *Science of being and art of living: Transcendental meditation.* New York: Plume.

Zakrzewski, V. (2013, October 2). Can mindfulness make us better teachers? *Greater Good Magazine.* Retrieved from https://greatergood.berkeley.edu/article/item /can_mindfulness_make_us_better_teachers

Zalaznick, M. (2017, May). Mindfulness exercises for children. *District Administration.* Retrieved from https://www.districtadministration.com/article/mindfulness -makes-difference-school

Zenner, C., Hernleben-Kurz, S., & Walach, H. (2014, June). Mindfulness-based interventions in schools—a systematic review and meta-analysis. *Frontiers of Psychology, 30*(5). Retrieved from https://www.ncbi.nlm.nih.gov/pmc/articles /PMC4075476/

Index

Note: The letter *f* following a page number denotes a figure, the letter *g* denotes a glossary entry.

About the Author

**Thomas Armstrong,** PhD, is an educator, psychologist, and writer who has worked in education for more than 45 years. He is the author of 18 books, including the ASCD books *Multiple Intelligences in the Classroom, Neurodiversity in the Classroom, The Power of the Adolescent Brain, The Best Schools, The Multiple Intelligences of Reading and Writing, ADD/ ADHD Alternatives in the Classroom,* and *Awakening Genius in the Classroom.* He is also the author of *7 Kinds of Smart, In Their Own Way, The Power of Neurodiversity,* and *The Myth of the ADHD Child.* His books have been translated into 28 languages, including Russian, Arabic, Chinese, and Spanish. In the last 30 years, he has delivered more than a thousand workshops, seminars, and keynote addresses in 44 states and 29 countries on 6 continents. He has written for *Family Circle, Ladies Home Journal, Parenting, The AMA Journal of Ethics,* and numerous other magazines and journals. He can be reached by e-mail at thomas@institute4learning.com or through his website: www.institute4learning.com, which includes further information about his books, presentations, articles, and speaking schedule.

Related ASCD Resources

At the time of publication, the following resources were available (ASCD stock numbers in parentheses).

Print Products

All Learning Is Social and Emotional: Helping Students Develop Essential Skills for the Classroom and Beyond, by Nancy Frey, Douglas Fisher, and Dominique Smith (#119033)

Creating a Trauma-Sensitive Classroom (Quick Reference Guide), by Kristin Souers and Pete Hall (#QRG118054)

Cultivating Habits of Mind (Quick Reference Guide), by Arthur L. Costa and Bena Kallick (#QRG117098)

Discipline with Dignity: How to Build Responsibility, Relationships, and Respect in Your Classroom, 4th ed., by Richard Curwin, Allen Mendler, and Brian Mendler (#118018)

The Formative Five: Fostering Grit, Empathy, and Other Success Skills Every Student Needs, by Thomas Hoerr (#116043)

Fostering Resilient Learners: Strategies for Creating a Trauma-Sensitive Classroom, by Kristin Souers and Pete Hall (#116014)

The New Teacher's Companion: Practical Wisdom for Succeeding in the Classroom, by Gini Cunningham (#109051)

Nurturing Habits of Mind in Early Childhood: Success Stories from Classrooms Around the World, by Arthur L. Costa and Bena Kallick (#119017)

The Power of the Adolescent Brain: Strategies for Teaching Middle and High School Students, by Thomas Armstrong (#116017)

For up-to-date information about ASCD resources, go to www.ascd.org. You can search the complete archives of *Educational Leadership* at www.ascd.org/el.

ASCD myTeachSource®

Download resources from a professional learning platform with hundreds of research-based best practices and tools for your classroom at http://myteachsource.ascd.org/

For more information, send an e-mail to member@ascd.org; call 1-800-933-2723 or 703-578-9600; send a fax to 703-575-5400; or write to Information Services, ASCD, 1703 N. Beauregard St., Alexandria, VA 22311-1714 USA.